FABLED LAND | TIMELESS RIVER

FABLED LAND | TIMELESS RIVER

life along the mississippi

Stephen Feldman
Van Gordon Sauter

Chicago
Quadrangle Books
1970

Fabled Land, Timeless River.

Copyright © 1970 by Stephen Feldman and Van Gordon Sauter. All rights reserved, including the right to reproduce this book or portions thereof in any form. For information, address: Quadrangle Books, Inc., 12 East Delaware Place, Chicago 60611. Manufactured in the United States of America. Published simultaneously in Canada by Burns and MacEachern Ltd., Toronto.

Library of Congress Catalog Card Number: 70-116086
SBN 8129-0154-1

Typography and Binding Design by genesis incorporated

For P.G.B. and A.R.B., with increasing appreciation——*V.G.S.*

For all my parents, with special thanks to Julie Lohn and Mickey Pallas——*S.F.*

The Mississippi begins quietly enough, with a brief and uncharacteristic display of humility, in northern Minnesota, about 115 miles from Canada, at Itasca State Park. Although some cartographers now place the site of the river's origin at Little Elk Lake, the forces of tradition and tourism have deemed it more convenient to establish their marker and parking lots about five miles away at one of the arms of the Y-shaped Lake Itasca. At this point no more than a small stream, the Mississippi falls away from the lake, drops a few inches over some large stones, then dashes back into a blur of weaving willow thickets in its escape from the legislated tranquillity of the state park for the harsher reality of life downstream.

Lake Itasca was discovered and named in 1832 by Henry Rowe Schoolcraft. A frontier Renaissance man of sorts, Schoolcraft has been variously regarded as an anthropologist, scholar, mineralogist, explorer, ethnographer, author, politician, and Indian agent. In 1832 he set out to abate the hostilities between the Chippewa and the Sioux in the upper reaches of Minnesota as well as to fulfill a long-held ambition to discover the true source of the Mississippi. Financed by the War Department, he resolutely led a flotilla of heavily burdened canoes into the northern waters. On July 13 the crew came upon a body of clear water known to the Indians as Elk Lake. Schoolcraft promptly declared it the source of the Mississippi and dutifully planted an American flag on an island in the lake. After the briefest of ceremonies and exploration, Schoolcraft the explorer became Schoolcraft the Indian agent, and the flotilla pushed on to calm the warring Indians.

No quotation from Schoolcraft today graces the site of the Mississippi's source. Instead, driving into the parking lot at Lake Itasca you are greeted by a sign more in the spirit of George Babbitt than of a nineteenth-century scholar-adventurer. The sign proclaims: "In life as in baseball, it is the number of times you reach home safely that counts."

Buoyed by that inspirational message, you proceed down a trail to the river, strikingly beautiful and in handsome contrast to much that is to follow. The lake is tranquil and blue, rimmed by a solid phalanx of fir trees. Out toward the middle is the island upon which Schoolcraft planted his flag. The water that slides from the lake over the rocks into the stream is clear—you can see eighteen inches to the bottom. No sludge. No oil slicks. No soggy cardboard washed up on the banks. In the distance, barely moving, yet so clear as to seem almost a stage prop, is a solitary canoe. The scene is so fine in its purity that yet another sign about litter control offers no distraction.

The river—it is really still a stream, but the maps grant it immediate maturity—doesn't tarry but strikes out, making a series of jogs and bends that are slight premonitions of the massive convolutions that develop downstream. The brush forms a protective gauntlet for the water, and it is only a brief walk along the stream before your shoes sink into the black mud. Most people content themselves with the tricky task of leaping across the stones in the water, thus earning the privilege of saying, "I walked across the Mississippi River."

A doctor and his wife, clutching their worn copies of Peterson's *Field Guide to the Birds,* stalk a Blackburnian Warbler through the trees. "Thank goodness, birds get used to people," the doctor declares. "One of the best places I've found for birds is Prospect Park in Brooklyn. Terribly crowded." With that the doctor and his wife, whose own most distinctive marking is ankle-length white sox, pursue their warbler.

A boy and girl, cans of Grain Belt beer in hand, stumble from the trees, wander briefly through the area in search of "the other people from the prom," then disappear back into the woods. A rackety school bus disgorges a flock of giggling girls who run madly for the water. Trailing behind is the plumpest of the crowd. a young lady in brightly checkered Bermudas, munching on potato chips.

Lake Itasca, Minnesota

Mostly, families come. Couples with two or three children traveling in station wagons and four-door sedans, bags and containers strapped to the roofs, rear seats littered with blankets and cracker boxes and tour guides. With sites of greater beauty and lesser congestion available elsewhere, what brings them to the small clearing in the park? Most people, it seems, like a precise order to things—a defined beginning and a recognizable end. If one has seen the Mississippi River, and in some way been affected by it, then one should have a knowledge of its origin; and there is something deeply satisfying about seeing the rivulet that sets in motion the great river that flows on for 2,500 miles.

The river quickly escapes the park, and then eludes a row of archaic wooden motel cabins, one of which is identified as the "Honeymoon Cabin," and an "Eat—Beer—Gas" joint which invites tourists to "See our bear cub." While the pastoral park tends to be ringed by commercial opportunism, the river's path is too devious and unpredictable for the road and the scrambling merchants to keep up with. It soon grows to twenty feet in width, passing through farmyards and stands of timber. In the spring, the countryside is soft and inviting, though the land is dotted by the lonely wreckage of abandoned farms, which lend an isolated, unreal quality to the remaining occupied farmhouses.

Near the town of Bemidji the river skirts about one hundred feet behind a vacant home, whose only historical context is a twisted 1949 "Minnesota Centennial" auto license plate. The road that leads back to the two-story tangle of a house is overgrown with weeds; the ruts themselves seem to be leveling out, as though the land were anxious to erase its own blight.

The house was built so that the kitchen and the upstairs bedrooms overlooked the river, which rushes from a lake, takes a straight course behind the house, and then disappears around a knoll. Crumbling steps now preclude a view from the second floor. The house is beyond saving; the wood has turned a moribund gray. Only the bright red chimney brick can match the intensity of the green grass and blue river. A few lilacs have pushed through the rusted bottom of a wash pail, which is surrounded by bits of glass and the legs, still upright, of what used to be a kitchen chair. These are the only remains of the family that once lived here. Down the road a young mother, preoccupied with her children, knew very little about the deserted home. "I understand an old man and his wife lived there. The man died and the woman moved away. There was a son, I think." Her own yard was alive with children and dogs and shiny equipment. Her man was out plowing. There was nothing transient about her life, her family, her farmhouse. The rubble nearby was without significance for her.

The river splashes into Lake Bemidji at the town of Bemidji, which is in the heart of Paul Bunyan country. At the edge of the lake sits a huge statue of the lumberman and his ox. It is next to an amusement park, which is next to a National Guard armory, which is next to a museum, which is near a stand selling "Bunyanburgers." A Bemidji store offers, among other things, a moving statue of an Indian, a stuffed lobo wolf that in legend is said to have killed one thousand deer, fishing licenses, native wild rice, deerskin gloves, leather hippie trousers, white chocolate, and psychedelic posters—something for everyone in this supermarket of tourism. The town itself is an amiable community, with a state college nestled in its rolling hills, and small, tidy homes. It is the upper Midwest at its most attractive.

The river flows east from Lake Bemidji, spreading out now to nearly two hundred feet wide, and moves into another series of lakes: Wolf, Andrusia, Cass, and Winnibigoshish. This is Chippewa Indian country. Every American by now has read the grim statistics of contemporary American Indian life—40 per cent unemployment with widespread underemployment, dilapidated housing, at least 30 per cent illiteracy, tuberculosis incidence seven times the national average, only two-thirds the life expectancy of other Americans, and less than a third of the national per capita income. The statistics pale beside the reality.

Bemidji, Minnesota [and facing page]

West of Wolf Lake a small wooden hovel plastered with asbestos paper sits off a road, adjoining the river. A stocky Indian woman in tall rubber boots, just returned from fishing with her children, stands in the entrance behind a badly punctured screen door—one which at best might pose a psychological barrier against insects. Her blind mother shuffles cautiously across the buckled linoleum floor to caution the daughter about talking to strangers. A sister with a heart condition and a brother unable to work because of a bad back live in smaller shacks near the building. The brother, who has been making a feeble attempt to cut firewood for winter, walks over and listens to his sister talk about their grandfather, who died in 1943 at the age of ninety-two. "He told us about the payments we would get from the government for the minerals and timber. If they would only live up to their treaty, things would be good for us." The brother nods.

"I don't think they will ever do anything. The Indian commission people come out here, but they see only the Indians in town with running water. They don't come out here. We have to pay $3.50 for a fishing license."

The brother, without a word, turns and trudges back to the woodpile, followed by a nephew. The man takes two or three whacks at a log, then stops to flex his aching back muscles. The boy watches intently —which is probably a good idea, for statistics indicate that someday he will probably be in the same predicament.

Not far away, where the Mississippi unites Andrusia and Cass lakes, there is an old Chippewa burial site overgrown with weeds and dotted by birch trees. The graves are covered by long, narrow houselike structures about two feet tall, apparently designed to house the spirits of the departed. These are covered with thick layers of moss, and most have collapsed. In this bizarre ghost town the plastic flowers seem more adept at surviving the elements than the wooden houses intended for eternity. Some of the newer constructions are elaborate, with shingles and shiny strips of metal across the spines of the roofs. In front of a recent one is a humble tombstone, which states:

Pvt. Curtis Leslie Hardy. Minnesota. Pvt. U.S. Marine Corps. Nov. 10, 1943–July 24, 1968.

It was a chilly fall afternoon, the opening day of duck-hunting season, and even though the gray sky was deserted there was an occasional burst of gunfire. Did Curtis Leslie Hardy, American Indian, Chippewa tribe, die at Hue or Con Thien? How irrelevant a death in Southeast Asia seems for an Indian! The house above Private Hardy's grave brought back memories of the little houses on stilts—containing joss sticks and miniature rice bowls—that many Vietnamese maintained for the wandering spirits of their departed elders. Marines sometimes mistook these for stakes intended to impale descending U.S. helicopters; they knocked them to the ground, much to the dismay of the Vietnamese. Private Hardy would have known better.

Suddenly a car burst over the hill and, hugging the center of the road, sped down toward the short bridge over the Mississippi. It was an old car, more suited to a demolition derby than to regular driving. Along its sides were broad stripes of rust, replacing long-gone strips of chrome.

The car, its rear end fishtailing, squealed to a stop, and the three front-seat occupants lurched forward like lifeless dummies in a traffic safety film. They were teen-age girls—loose, grinning, their teeth small and bright in broad brown faces framed by long black hair. Each had a six-pack container of beer. One girl began to giggle, and the driver pushed nervously at the accelerator. The car balked and then sputtered forward, down the center of the road. With the hunters firing away at decoys or imagined spots in the sky, and three drunk Indian girls careening off toward oblivion, it seemed worthwhile to learn more of Curtis Leslie Hardy.

There is a small grocery store down the road from the river. It is immaculately white. The driveway is lined by small whitewashed rocks. A short, squat woman with fluffy hair and a dour demeanor stood behind the meat counter. Her husband was in the back room watching a World Series game.

Cass Lake, Minnesota [and following pages]

"Did we know Curtis Leslie Hardy? We knew Leslie about eighteen years. Did he ever come by the store? He very seldom left it. He came here because he was welcome. He had the run of the house. We met him as a young boy when we came up to my sister's to visit. We were from Mankato. We've been living here going on four years. He lived across the road. Lived with his mother. He was a tall boy, a very nice and neat boy. Bring out that picture of Leslie," she yelled back to her husband. A man walked out with a framed picture and quickly returned to the game. Leslie was a nice-looking boy.

"Was he killed in Vietnam?"

"No. There was something about him being *AWOL*. But he told us he thought better of that and he went back. It must have been straightened out because he was buried with the flag. No. He wasn't a drinker or a fighter. During the summer if he got a wee bit dirty he would go down to the river to get clean.

"On the day it happened I said, 'My, but you're a dirty boy.' 'Don't worry,' he said, 'I'll be back.' Down to the river he went. He never came back. Three times a year he went out for a good time—his birthday, New Year's Eve, and some other occasion. He was to be married the day he was buried.

"He was bathing when he was hit by a boat being run by a sixteen-year-old boy. Killed him right away. I couldn't understand it. As a child, Leslie went to church. His mother told me afterward that he had made the request to be buried as an Indian if anything ever happened to him. 'I'm a full-blooded Indian,' he told her. He was. And he was one of the few who was a good boy. He had one of the biggest services we've ever seen around here. And he was buried as a pagan."

The woman, handling the picture very carefully, returned it to the back room where the game was still playing on the television. There wasn't much else for the woman to say. Curtis Leslie Hardy, a Marine, a pagan, was a good man and died young. It would have been irrelevant for him to have died in Vietnam. It seemed even more irrelevant to die while taking a bath in the Mississippi.

Cass Lake is a small town which seems to have more churches than stores. It is redolent of heavy woolen jackets and self-reliance and love of the land. A local service club maintains an outdoor display case where the largest fish caught in nearby lakes are put on display. A colorful map designed for tourists has one entry under entertainment: American Legion Club. The citizens are chauvinistic and energetic, and the local paper faithfully records their endeavors:

"A farewell party for the Jim Blombergs, who are leaving next week for Soddy, Tennessee, was held Wednesday night at the Farris School. Pot-luck lunch was served and the Blombergs were presented a purse of money by their friends."

"We wish to sincerely thank the people of the Cass Lake & Laporte Community who came out and helped search for Simon Goodwin, who was lost in the woods while hunting. Especially do we thank the ladies of Laporte who served lunch and the Hubbard County Sheriff's office that directed the search. The family of Simon Goodwin." The search party, marshaled by the sounding of a fire-alarm siren, found Goodwin in a swampy area. Except for a bad chill and soggy clothes, the seventy-three-year-old partridge hunter was in good shape.

"Stanley Meads has received credentials as an official trapper who can collect bounty on predators he traps and tags. This region has been hard hit by wolves for several years, both livestock and deer being victims."

Some Minnesota residents regard Cass Lake as a rough town where the Indians raise hell on Friday night, then sleep it off for six days while the white residents effect repairs and brace up for the next weekend. The Cass Lake police chief frowned at such comments. "We run a law-and-order town," said Andrew "Red" Holes, chief of the three-man police force. "It's not as bad as it used to be. It gets busy on Friday night, but it's teen-agers who give us the most trouble. But that's true anywhere. It's a lot harder in this business now. I can't ask your name unless I read Miranda." The chief cleared his throat. "And for instance, sir," he began in a derisive voice, "if you don't want to answer me, I can't question you unless you have a lawyer, or I could easily have a lawsuit on my hands."

The chief, who has an office behind a small courtroom, would, in spite of Miranda and Friday nights, rather be a police chief in Cass Lake than anything else. "Up here you don't have to be afraid to drink the water straight from the Mississippi. You go down to the Twin Cities and you can hardly drink the water straight from the tap because of all the chlorine. If the wind is right down there, you can smell the Twin Cities ten miles out."

There are many in Cass Lake who don't share the chief's euphoria. While most Indians in the area tend toward the lethargic, a few now talk of "red power" as a means of escaping what they contend to be real economic, social, and governmental repression. Elmer David Jones is a Cass Lake Indian leader who claims to have experienced discrimination. "I went to school here in Cass Lake. They made me feel ashamed to be an Indian. I don't think my kids should get anything special, but they should be treated equal. Now we are trying to get on the school board. We don't want teachers to downgrade Indians."

Jones also says there is discrimination in employment, and that the federal and state governments are callous to the special needs of the Indian population. "The Bureau of Indian Affairs' idea is to assimilate us into the white population. To an extent, we should be more assimilated. But at the same time I think the Indian should hang onto his culture." Jones talks urgently about preserving Indian culture and identity while he sits in front of a huge television set, glancing occasionally at a World Series game. His house has all the trappings—even down to a portrait of John F. Kennedy—of contemporary blue-collar America.

Jones talks—not with an angry militancy, but with a quiet wishfulness—of fighting the governmental bureaucracies and even the corporations, which he believes to be smothering what few traces of Indian self-assertion exist. It is reminiscent of sitting in dingy little ghetto stores about fifteen years ago, drinking a Royal Crown while the blacks talked about someday being free.

Robert Charles Knight is a *VISTA* volunteer who works with the local Indian reservation business council. He is a twenty-three-year-old Colgate graduate from Binghamton, New York, and lives in a partially reconverted garage. He wears a Beatle cap adorned by a peace button; the wall in his living room has a Frederic Remington print and a Eugene McCarthy campaign poster. Most of the *VISTA* programs with the Indians in this portion of Minnesota have come to very little. Knight's group, however, has successfully organized, among other things, a literacy program, legal aid services, and a teen center. In the process it is obvious that Robert Knight has learned a lot about himself and a portion of the world his parents didn't know about and very probably couldn't comprehend. "The Indians ask only two things," Knight says, "sensitivity and a willingness to learn."

The river, still clear and sparkling, flows southwest from the lakes into Grand Rapids, a neat little town whose name derives from a rapids long since replaced by a dam. A paper company settled at the river's edge because it offered the vast quantities of power and pure water required to grind logs into the pulp which is needed for paper. In return for its generous provision of power and water, the Mississippi here receives its first dose of industrial pollution. The plant itself is pristine; directly across the river is a small park and a charming residential area. But you can stand amid the birch trees in the park, in this unusual blending of industry and homes and nature, and watch a foul-colored stream of water gush from factory pipes into the river.

The state pollution control agency claims the firm is initiating corrective steps, but that is of little significance to William Koski, who lives several miles downstream. The Mississippi is his front yard, and in flood season he used to be able to fish from his porch. Today Koski finds little joy in the river or its fish.

William Koski is a short man who wears an old sweat-stained fedora with the brim scissored off. There is something slow, even discouraged, about his walk and manner of speech. Somehow the dream passed him by. "I've been here since 1940. My wife and me. No children. We got chased out of Dakota by the depression and drought. But it's been a depression here, too. I've made a living. Nothing more. I thought it was pretty nice when we first lived here. Now it's just a place to live. There's supposed to be 137 acres. I can't find them. The river moves. There's no permanent pasture. It's under water half the time. When we first moved here I caught fish. Good fish. But about '46 was the last fish I caught. They weren't eatable. The flesh was yellow. Wasn't worth eating. It was nice having fish when you were short on money. It would be nice now." But Koski can't think of many nice things these days. He finds the river malicious, the fish fouled by something he doesn't understand. "They do something to the water up there," he says, pointing toward Grand Rapids. He gets a poor return from his four cattle and thirty sheep. He walked, slowly, back to his house. It was the walk of a sixty-eight-year-old man who has been run into the ground.

A few miles on, Archie Carlisle, who is a farmer, delights in the river. "You can always find a little excitement about this river. You see all kinds of animals, even those big old turtles." Archie and Duchess, his coon hound, were trooping along a bluff above the river. The Mississippi was now flexing its growing muscles, butting into Archie's pasture and further isolating an island in mid-river. "You don't notice it, but that river is changing things around here every day. Suddenly you look and wonder, where did that land go. It's gone and you didn't even notice enough to say goodbye."

Archie lives across the road from the river in a small house. Next to his house are sheds where he keeps farm equipment, traps, and animal skins. "I trap beaver, otter, mink, muskrat, fox, wolves, bobcat, and bear. There's a lot of bear. Occasionally you can take a young sheep around here. I make about $600 from the traps. That helps. I got about 190 acres and forty-five head of cattle. In a way, it's not good land. It's sandy and doesn't hold strength."

Grand Rapids, Minnesota [and facing page]

Archie is proud of this land, his trapping, and his relationship with the river. But he too laments the decline of the fish. "Ah, the fish we used to get here were good. How they've changed! They have that paper mill and sewage disposal. Down here the fish taste like they came from a muddy slough. In the summer the river gets a lot of white flaky stuff in it. Above Grand Rapids it's clear as a bell. But down here it is different. Should be the same all the way along."

He is not the type of man to go complaining. There isn't the time, and he believes someone, somewhere, is trying to do something about the bad fish and sewage and flaky stuff. "This land has been good to me. I try to be good with it, too. I only kill to eat or sell. If I see a bear or a timber wolf—I can see them right out the back window there—I wouldn't shoot them. I like to have them around. It's good for us."

The Mississippi spends nearly a third of its life in Minnesota, initially moving sideways, at angles, developing its path south. Little towns—the might-have-been towns stunted by the quirks of history or the whims of man—dot the route. Conceived by the river, nurtured for a time by the railroads, with the urbanization of America they are now falling into decay. Once they serviced the farmers, whose main contact with the outside world is now through the highways and piped in by television. The residents in these towns tend to be old, very friendly, and generally have a sense of sympathy for the young, engendered by the feeling that youth are inheriting and helping a life that is careening toward disaster.

Such a town is Palisade. Lumberjacks used to herd logs down the river past Palisade. Boats tied up there to unload supplies for the farmers. They were replaced by the railroads. The train station, with its clean and precise lines, is still there, and on the sidings are cars loaded with logs. But the scene is stationary, a museum piece frozen in history. Palisade itself is now threadbare.

Tom is young and handsome, with deep blue eyes and light brown hair. The bandage on his left hand covers scarred and bloated flesh. "It happened at An Hoa. They started dropping mortars. I just got hit by a stray round. There's no feeling there." Unlike the forty-five who responded to Lincoln's call, Tom joined the Marines out of boredom. "I just wanted to get away. Vietnam's no place to be if you're married and have a wife. But I want to go back. I liked it over there, driving a truck. But then I like it here, too. Particularly in the winter." He puts a Sergeant Barry Sadler "Green Berets" record on a phonograph. "I like these woods in the winter. I like to run out through the snow." His mother comes up behind him and affectionately squeezes his shoulders. "My boy always liked the snow," she says. "Could be a blizzard out there and I've had to go out and get his butt back home." Tom, his Vietnam souvenir painfully obvious, leans back in his chair and looks up at his mother. He smiles, blushing at her concern.

Back out in the yard, the woman expresses her opinions about the river. "My boy James—I had eleven children—was drowned in the river last week. He went fishing and the boat tipped. Jim just wasn't thinking like he should have been. We always taught respect for the river. It was nothing to be played with." She frowns and goes back to her yard work while the sounds of Sergeant Sadler's patriotic music filter through the door under the drooping flag.

While Police Chief Holes and the bloodhounds may be able to sniff the Twin Cities ten miles out, Minneapolis and St. Paul appear only gradually, with suburban housing and a few industrial plants hinting at their presence. The cities, particularly Minneapolis, are strikingly attractive, with an air of initiative and enterprise pleasantly devoid of the usual urban haste and smells. The weather can be painfully bitter in the winter, though. The Twin Cities blithely shrug off blizzards that would incapacitate other metropolitan areas for days. The plains to the west send in waves of smothering hot air during the summer, forcing the residents to nearby parks (Minneapolis has one acre of park land for every eighty-five inhabitants) and lakes (there are thirty within thirty minutes of St. Paul). In the fall and spring, however, there is a tranquillity to both communities, which seem to relish the river, the lakes, and the pine forests to the north.

—At the Fort Ripley National Guard Camp, an imposing tank is perched on a hill formed by a bulldozer, its snout pointing toward the highway. A beer can lies next to a tank tread.

—At Little Falls young boys, receiving unsolicited advice from elderly onlookers, fish in the river above a hydroelectric plant. Below the plant the water is sullied by a brownish taint. No one is fishing there.

—A housing development: "Via Riviera. Choice river lots. Boating. Financing. Restricted." In an attempt to discover what is restricted, a visitor knocks at the door of a Via Riviera residence. The woman inside hushes the children and refuses to answer the door. The visitor leaves when she starts making a phone call. Some police don't understand such curiosity.

Farther on, pastoral scenes diminish and billboards, gas stations, and signs pointing toward expressways become more frequent. Suddenly a huge church appears on a hill. It overlooks the small town of Dayton. "This is a proud community," says an elderly woman whose forefathers helped shape the town. "When Lincoln called the men to arms, forty-five from the town volunteered."

Up the street a heavy-set woman was working on the small yard in front of her house over whose entrance flew an American flag. "We bought the flag the first day of May," the woman said. "We were up in Big Lake shopping when my husband saw it and decided to buy it. It was the first flag we ever bought. We had just never thought of a flag. The day we put the flag up the Marine came at night and told us of Tom. About his hand. He's inside."

Camp Ripley, Minnesota

Gus Watson sits on a wooden bench in the front yard of a Palisade home that overlooks the Mississippi. He pokes small holes in the earth with his white cane while reciting a litany about the glory of past years. He is pushing seventy, and the years, for all their glory, have ceased to be generous to him. He is blind; his body is lumpy and tired. Even his cane is held together with tape. His clothes—pants, yellow suspenders, and checkered shirt—have all faded to a uniform drabness. But the intensity of his memories has not diminished. "I was born four miles west of the river. My family came up from West Virginia and took 160 acres as homesteaders. She was rough in those days. On the homestead you went to the city only three times a year. Did you know that? You took the ox team in good weather, the horses and a sled in the winter. In the high-water days you didn't go at all. These families today"—he raised his cane into the air, moving it back and forth—"have cars and the kids will drive four or five times a day to the stores. And school. Whenever we went to school it was through the woods for two miles. On foot!"

Watson worked as a logger in Minnesota and Oregon, and in 1927 returned to settle along the Mississippi. "I went right into the woods logging. The men were pretty tough in the old days. Not mean, except perhaps when they went into town once or twice a year and put in a couple of days." In those days the loggers built little movable camps—bunkhouses, toolsheds, kitchens—on rafts and moved them down the Mississippi. "Any time you wanted to cross the river you grabbed a log and went across. Wasn't a big thing. But the river's going to pieces now. It's filling up with trash. In those days we kept the river clean. In those days you took all the fish you wanted. Today there ain't any comparison. You can hardly get down the river with a canoe, let alone a boat. Things are changing for the worse—the weather, everything. The people are pulling out. Where you used to have five farmers you now have two. The old farms are growing up. I think people will end up starving. You go down to the city and get me ten people who can come up here to the woods and make a living. Can't do it. Look at me, all my five kids are in factories. I liked the old days. Those were the only days."

The Mississippi, with growing intensity, pushes toward Minneapolis and St. Paul. South of Brainerd, it is joined from the west by the Crow Wing River and nearly doubles in size. Increasingly now, the modern world begins to make its presence felt.

On the track side of the building, a tall window juts out from the structure, so the stationmaster can look up and down the tracks. The window is nearly covered by yellowed newspapers, dateline 1966, to ward off the sun. Gilio J. Baldovin now occupies the office, which has richly colored wooden furniture once common to train stations and post offices and general stores. The furniture is covered by a thick coat of dust, as are the dated railroad posters, one of which depicts a father instructing his son about the meaning of the stop signals at a train crossing. (Next to them is an automobile that predates Word War II.) After dusting off chairs for his visitors, Baldovin sits in a high-backed swivel chair in front of a desk with an old-fashioned telegraph ticker. At sixty he has only two years until retirement, when he plans to hunt and fish and just think about the good old days of railroading.

"I used to have ten, twelve, fourteen trains a day through here," he began. "Now it is one train going east, one going west. I used to sell tickets. I used to take telegrams. I used to handle the express. That's all gone. Express money orders are gone, too. There was also LCL, less-than-carload freight. That's gone. I guess you could call me a man of leisure."

With the exception of the two trains, Baldovin has little company at the Palisade station except in the winter, when the section crews come in to have lunch around an old black stove in the waiting room.

"I feel the railroad workers have been let down," Baldovin continued. "When we started, thirty years or so ago, working on the railroad gave you a place in the community. You were looked up to; you were a little better than the working man. Nowadays, though, you are a cog in the machine. The railroad has you right by the rear end." He got up from the chair and walked out to the platform. Tall grass grew between some of the tracks. It was quiet at the Palisade station. Nothing would move for a couple of hours. "It's a real tragedy," Baldovin said. "I don't know what will happen without the railroads."

Palisade, Minnesota

Twin Cities [and following page]

Minneapolis

Near the heart of downtown Minneapolis are the Falls of St. Anthony, the navigable head of the Mississippi. During the middle of the last century, this was an important stop on the fashionable tour taken by many Americans and continentals through the rustic upper Midwest. The falls have since been marshaled into a lock-and-dam system and seem almost tragically mechanized. Past the falls and the campus of the University of Minnesota, the Mississippi slips into a tree-lined gorge. The roads along either side of the river provide one of the most beautiful drives in urban America. At water level the cities fall out of view, except for the towers of a few high-rise buildings and the bridges spanning the river. To the south, Minnehaha Creek plunges over a fifty-foot falls (celebrated by Longfellow in his epic poem "Hiawatha") before joining the river.

At the meeting of the Mississippi and Minnesota rivers, historians are at work rebuilding Fort Snelling, one of the most colorful outposts on the upper river. In 1805 Lieutenant Zebulon Pike acquired the strategic bluff overlooking the merging of the two rivers, and the outpost was developed by Colonel Josiah Snelling, who made it a gem of civilization in the midst of the wilderness. Young officers from the East soldiered through the dense woods, protecting the fur trade and controlling the Indians, and then returned to their post, which was graced by gala socials comprised of splendid feasts and vibrant quadrilles. In 1823 the Steamboat *Virginia* moved into the northern portion of the river, passing through the huge rock bluffs. It shared the river only with Indian canoes and the fur traders' flat-bottomed bateaux. On May 10 the *Virginia* reached the lonely army outpost. Her successful voyage triggered a flood of river traffic north to the Falls of St. Anthony. The arrival of more white men and their commerce further diminished the options of the Indians. In 1862, after an abortive Sioux uprising, the fort witnessed one of the most symbolic moments in the history of the river when two of the rebellious Sioux leaders, Medicine Bottle and Shakopee, were executed at the fort. As the hangman prepared to drape a black cape over the head of Shakopee, the chief raised his arm, looked down the river, and declared: "As the white man comes in, the Indian goes out." At that very moment the shrill whistle of a locomotive sounded in the valley below—the first steam-driven train had arrived.

Hastings, Minnesota

Above the Twin Cities, the land is wild and wooded; below, the Mississippi drains a wide and fertile prairie. The river itself is lined by soaring sandstone bluffs. Coming over a hill into Hastings, one senses for the first time the essential river town. The hill is dominated by two old homes—a plain though sturdy stone structure with a widow's walk, and a more elaborate octagonal house. Both hark up images of entrepreneurs anxious to bring the style and comfort of the East to the primitive frontier. A New England–style courthouse, having an air of dignity and authority lacking in the glass and stainless steel of more contemporary courthouses, rises above the downtown area. Two blocks from the Mississippi is a sagging old hotel with a wide front porch and pillars against which one can lean while taking in the first traces of morning sun. The three sisters who developed it into a showplace are gone. The last, a woman formidable in bulk and vocabulary, was evicted because of legal and credit problems. Refusing to walk out of her hotel, she was carried out on a cot by the sheriff and his deputies. Only a floor-to-ceiling mirror in the lobby now hints at the gilt which once typified the hotel.

Although the hotel is fading and the octagonal house has been divided into apartments, the town of Hastings is thriving. The population has more than doubled in the last fifteen years, and many people now commute to Minneapolis and St. Paul. But proximity to the big cities has its problems. Hastings residents were complaining about a fight at a drive-in between some local boys and a gang from the Twin Cities. A bad omen, they said. But things haven't really changed. They would do well to read the first edition, in 1857, of the local paper, a journal dedicated in those days to "territorial interests, politics, education, news, commerce, literature, poetry and amusement." It noted a "serious collision" on the levee between some citizens of Hastings and the officers and crew of the U.S. Mail Steam Packet *Galena*. One week later the editor recorded rumors of "gunfire in the Western Hotel." "We trust," he wrote, "this report is erroneous, as such occurrences reflect no credit on the city and debase the individuals immediately concerned."

But the cities also bring a more subtle form of violence—pollution. "The water around here isn't fit for recreation," said one Hastings resident. "From Minneapolis to Red Wing you just can't safely use the Mississippi for fun. One of the cities up there sometimes dumps raw sewage in the river. If you or I walked down to the river and squatted to put some raw sewage into the water, you know damn well what would happen. But a city can do it. And nothing happens."

A few miles south of Hastings is one of the twenty-seven locks and dams maintained for navigational purposes between Minneapolis and St. Louis by the U.S. Army Corps of Engineers. Earl R. Flynn, who is fifty-seven, works at Lock and Dam Number Three. "My father was a commercial fisherman around here," he said. "I was born on the river right up there where you see the atomic power plant going up. I used to be a trapper hereabouts, but it's all played out. Has been for about fifteen years. The mink is gone. So are the raccoons. I even gave up my coon dogs. And it doesn't pay to take out a license on ducks. When I was nineteen or twenty they would rise off the water here like a cloud. The sky would be black with them. Nothing now.

"With the cities you can't help this happening. They have all that cement up there in the cities. The salt they put down on the streets in the winter, and the oil and gas, it washes right into the water. Over by the dam the foam is pink with detergents."

Since Lock and Dam Number Three is far off the road and needs round-the-clock supervision, the government has provided two neat white clapboard houses with green shutters for the lockmaster and his assistant. There are toys on the well-trimmed lawns, and cement walks lead to the locks and control buildings. Eugene Schuppel, who manages the operation at Number Three, has been on the locks for eighteen years. He chews simultaneously on a cigar and a toothpick while watching a tug push a line of barges toward his lock. "This is my life. I've always liked the water. You can say I'm a water rat, and it's true—that saying that once you get around the river you tend to stay with it. People think that all a lockmaster does is just sit around and wait for the boats. I should live that long. Look around this place. We put in 85,000 sandbags in spring because of the floods. And from the day school's out until Labor Day there are little boats all the time."

Pushing twelve barges, three across and four from front to back, the *Kay A* was lining up in front of the lock, her red hull rising up like an angry snout. In the middle of the front center barge a pole flew a white flag, and crewmen in orange jackets stood at the front corners. The barges were 105 feet across, the lock 110 feet wide—a margin of five feet. With a roar of her engines, the *Kay A* began to churn water and shove the barges into the lock. A grating noise sounded as the right side of the front barge slid against the lock.

"Hold back and straighten out," shrieked Schuppel, pacing along the side of the lock with the concern of a father teaching his daughter to park his new car. After a series of maneuvers, the *Kay A* was securely in the lock, prepared for yet another step in the trek toward the Twin Cities, with a load of grain to be hauled back downstream.

"The maintenance work is year round," Schuppel said, examining the area where the barge ground against the lock. Has there been any change in the Mississippi during his years on the locks? "The change is pollution. In 1952 or '53 there were so many winter fishermen here you could hardly get down the road to get to work. Now you see one or two. The water looks dirtier all the time. It's just that the country's going so fast they neglect things. And things depreciate. Then they get to the things that should have been done years earlier. Some day they'll get the pollution work done. I hope. We used to get sunfish here all the time. Not a one now."

Along the river, people like Archie Carlisle and Eugene Schuppel talk about "they" getting things done. By "they," of course, is meant the distant, expensive, and always tardy government.

At Red Wing the Mississippi broadens to form Lake Pepin, the most strikingly beautiful portion of the river. Twenty-two miles long, from one to two-and-a-half miles wide, the lake is framed by towering cliffs. William Jennings Bryan once said this lake "ought to be visited in the summer by every poet and painter in the land." On the Wisconsin side, approximately halfway down the lake, is Maiden Rock Point, also known inevitably as "Lover's Leap," from which an Indian maiden allegedly hurled herself when ordered to marry a brave she didn't love. The story lacks credibility if for no other reason than that the precipice has eluded high school seniors who scrawled "Class of '69" across every broad piece of rock along the highways.

Years ago this country was populated by lumberjacks and raft pilots—men as venturesome and dramatic as those legendary figures who settled the boom towns of the West. After chopping down the trees and moving them along the tributaries to the Mississippi, the lumberjacks became rivermen and lashed the logs into huge "Mississippi rafts," some fifteen hundred feet long and three hundred feet wide, which were floated downstream to such towns as Hannibal and St. Louis. The pilot, his memory his only navigational aid, occupied a small shed at the bow of the raft. The cookshed was amidships, and the crew had a bunkhouse astern. By having the crew push in unison at various points along the length of the raft, the pilot could exert some control over its direction. It was a tricky business, made successful only by the "river sense" of the pilot and the fearlessness of the rivermen.

While the cook would lay in barrels of molasses and whiskey and flour, the men generally lived off the land, which was obligingly plentiful. One famous pilot is said to have caught a 180-pound channel catfish. Another pilot mounted a cannon on his raft and fired into the clouds of geese, killing dozens with a single round.

Pausing at river towns along the way, the crews created mayhem. Whoring, brawling, and cutting up generally, they leveled saloons and brought terror to the God fearing. One historian noted that "most people in the river towns were of the opinion that rafting was but a diversion for the crews; their true calling was battle, murder, and sudden death."

One of the great towns of the old days was Reads Landing, at the foot of Lake Pepin, where many of the rafts were formed. Lumberjacks, rivermen, wheat dealers, speculators, and immigrants gave it flavor, excitement, and aspiration. At the peak of the boom there were seventeen hotels to accommodate the river travelers. Like so many boom towns, Reads Landing today is fortunate just to be noted on the map. With the exception of a dingy museum, a historical marker, and some dated photographs in a filling station, Reads Landing is just another intersection.

There is a bait shop at the waterfront, and in spite of a handwritten "Closed" sign you can get a beer at the Anchor Bar. "Little Reads Landing got wiped out by the railroad," said a woman pumping gas at the intersection. "Most of the old buildings are gone. This town has more basements than anything else."

Reads Landing, Minnesota

Prairie du Chien, Wisconsin

The rivermen have been replaced by the tourists, who are generally better behaved and tend to pay for what they carry off. At Stockholm, on the Wisconsin side of Lake Pepin, Bennard Heinemann has created a combination museum, antique emporium, and junk shop to snare the tourists. Because of a better road and more complete historical markers, it is better to view Lake Pepin from the Wisconsin rather than the Minnesota side. Heinemann's shop is cluttered with clocks, tools, lawnmowers, dolls, pictorials, marbles, furniture, toys, and mounds of rusted metal of dubious utility. "Stockholm is like all these little river towns. Things have passed us by. We had the lumber. Then the fishing. Then the clams we sent off to the button factories. Plastic took care of that. Here, look at this fine old clam hook I have. But this certainly beats the pace of the city. I used to work down in LaCrosse. What a rat race. But they even catch up with you in a place like this. I need help here in the worst kind of way. But I don't think I can toe the mark in filling out the forms for Uncle Sam. If I get help, that means the forms; then I would need a bookkeeper." He pauses and places a World War II rationing book *(If You Don't Need It—Don't Buy It)* on a 1918 *Swamp Root Almanac*.

Heinemann walks from his musty store out onto the sheltered front porch to watch a light rain fall on the deserted street. There is a quiet, almost somber desolation about Stockholm. Did it ever know the joy and noise of a Fourth of July, a high school band marching toward a football stadium with wooden seats and glaring lights that turned the grass an eerie shade of green? Stockholm reflects the futility of a tired old man who has served adequately but without distinction; an old man waiting out his years uninterested in the world around him. Bennard Heinemann crouches down and begins working on the frame of a disemboweled power mower. A vacant lot stands between his store and an old John Deere implement store, which has been taken over by a blacksmith who keeps his anvil and furnace on the front porch. The lot is overgrown with weeds, which conceal sagging wagon wheels and hulks of abandoned machinery. The skeleton of a rusted tractor stands impotently at the rear of the lot.

Milton Lindgren, the blacksmith, was born in 1913 and has lived most of his life in Stockholm. He went to school with Heinemann. Lindgren's father learned the blacksmith trade in the old country. He immigrated to the Twin Cities, where he sharpened tools in the factories and changed shoes on horses that pulled ambulances. "He moved down to Stockholm because it was on a lake and had a railroad. If you have a railroad, you can get out." Lindgren works on tires, sharpens tools, and occasionally does some smithy work. "You have to. It's like milking a cow. If you don't do it now and then, your muscles can't take it."

Lindgren's clothes, like the building, are covered with soot. His life is centered on the store and the town. Some people talk of expressways to bring tourists to the lake and to towns like Stockholm. Lindgren isn't much interested. "Who are tourists? They are people who stop and buy gas and then drive four hundred miles till they need to buy more gas. There would be so many cars you couldn't get across the road."

An old man pumping gas around the corner is also uninterested in tourists and their dollars. "I was born on a farm in the sticks. My parents are poor. I'm poor. And that's how it goes."

Tourists and dusty antique shops, people and trinkets, undistinguishable from those 150 miles to the north or 150 miles to the south, seemed to dominate the small streets of Lansing, Iowa. None of the visitors paid any attention to Raymond Boardman, who was down at the river, at the edge of a soggy mud bank, shoveling fish from a flat-bottomed boat into wooden crates on a flimsy dock. His buddy was energetically scooping water from the boat with a shiny tin can, which, like the bloated bellies of the fish, glistened in the sun. It was hard work, bend-over work, and Boardman, who is in his early fifties, seemed too old for it.

"Who else is to do it?" he asked. "There ain't no young fishermen left. They won't go at it. They go into factories and make more a day. Why make twenty dollars a day on the river when you can get thirty to forty dollars a day in the city? Sometimes we don't get twenty. We'll be lucky to get fifteen today. I do sixty or seventy hours a week at this. During the winter we take a chain saw to the ice and go through thirty-four inches. And what do I get? I get nineteen cents a pound for sand sturgeon. You go into a store in Chicago and pay $4.50 a pound for it. There's no profit in that. At least not on my side. There's a monopoly in this fish business somewhere, but I can't put my finger on it. Everything goes up in this world except my fish. I'm getting the same price I got in the depression. And you ask why there's no youngster out here doing this work."

As Boardman ticked off his grievances, his helper increased the tempo of his bailing until a steady stream of water was sloshing overboard. He looked up and vigorously nodded his head in agreement with Boardman.

Downriver by several miles is the town of Marquette—a maze of worn buildings and a meager stretch of businesses. Near the center of the business section is the Marquette Hotel, which has large plate-glass windows rendered opaque by age and grime. A few plants struggle for survival in the window, and the registration desk is unmanned. Four old men play cards around a table; two men in railroad engineers' caps lounge in chairs against the wall, following the game's progress by reading the expressions on the faces of the players.

George Harrington, who is seventy-eight years old, is dominating the game, which is played so deliberately as to give the effect of being run in slow motion. He has on a gray hat, a heavy shirt which sags under the weight of a pocket filled with pens and pencils, and khaki trousers. Traces of white hair drop from beneath his hat to curl behind his ears. His main competitor in the game is Charley Peck, who is a mere seventy.

"The town hasn't changed much over the years," says Harrington, who opens a small cloth coin purse, drops in a few coins, then snaps it shut. "There's a nice motel and nightclub here now. But the big thing used to be the train depot. We had thirty-two passenger trains a day through here, and four or five hundred people working on the railroads.

Marquette, Iowa [and following pages]

"You know I can recall the flood of 1896," he continues. "I saved one hundred pigs that time. Lost thirty-nine." He deals a few cards.

After an interval of a few minutes Charley Peck looks up from his hand. "God damn, you're almost as old as I am." The men chuckle, and the onlookers glance at one another and grin.

"They built this hotel in 1906," Harrington goes on. "I ran the hotel for thirty-nine years. Every family in the town was railroad people except the merchants. There was one payday a month, and what a time it was. The highest pay was $75. They never saw a day less than twelve hours, you know. I got a dollar-ten a day when I worked on the section."

"More than you were worth," says Peck.

"You're right." The men, and Harrington with them, chuckle.

One of the men brings the game to a halt when he puts his cards face down on the table and walks over to an ashtray mounted on a wooden stand in the middle of the lobby. He taps out his pipe and gazes at the vacant street. "It was quite a town in those days. There wasn't a key in Marquette. People didn't need keys in those days. People were as fine as you could want to know. A little rough, perhaps, but bighearted."

"Saloons didn't need any keys," interrupts Peck. "They never closed. Remember the Klondike? What a place! We had the Klondike Saloon. The Bon Ton Saloon. The Hub Saloon. A lot of them. I was mayor here for twenty-five years. It was a good town. We had some problems when Wisconsin went wet and Iowa was dry. People would go over the river, get their bottles, and then come back here to get a train west. But if they ever went to sleep in that depot they would wake up without their booze. But this has been a good place to live. The smaller towns are all going down. I could see that when I sat in the mayor's chair. The people all want to get to the big supermarkets. They don't realize it's kinda handy to have small towns."

It is growing dark. Cars coming across the Mississippi bridge and up the street toward the hotel have their lights on. Time for old men to be home with their memories and television, and, if they are lucky, a woman in an apron to fix dinner. The room clicks with the sound of coin purses being opened and closed for the last time that day. The heavy coats—premature for that time of year—are pulled down from the wall hooks near a sign penciled on cardboard which reads, "Please Use the Ash Trays." There are no goodbyes, no need for them, for the game will resume the next day, as sure as Charley Peck will josh George Harrington about his age.

"We play cards there every afternoon," Harrington says during the ride home. "There isn't much else to do. It's gone by. For me and those gents." The subject of war comes up. "My grandfather was in the Civil War," Harrington says. "My father was in the Spanish War. I was in World War I, though I had a hard time getting into that one. I said to them, 'God damn it, I am as good as anyone you got.' They finally let me in. I had two boys in World War II. But I can't see this Vietnam war. Look, we got Cuba down there and we don't do anything about it. So why go to China?"

Harrington halts the flow of his opinions to direct the driver past the local nightclub, the old railroad roundhouse ("not one damned passenger train now"), and a weed-ridden baseball diamond. "Ah, this has been a good place and we've had some times. You know I really can recall that flood in 1896. I can see my mother now, sweeping the water out of the first floor with fish flopping on the floor." Harrington tips his hat as he gets out, and slowly walks away toward his dark house.

Like George Harrington, Marquette is in its twilight. The most important events in its life are past; there is now only a quiet resignation about the future. A few miles south is the town of McGregor—younger, more energetic, determined to lure and disarm the tourists who follow the Mississippi. At the edge of McGregor's small downtown park is a handsome old brick building with wide, fan-shaped windows. It was originally a steamboat shipping office, then later a post office—there are still tiny numbered mailboxes built into the wall. A young couple have since turned it into a restaurant, and rounds of pizza are passed from the kitchen through a window marked "Parcel Post—General Delivery." Nearby is the Sea Shell Shop. The window is cluttered with piles of multicolored seashells, some the size of a dime, others as large as a basketball. A frumpy woman sits in a folding chair in front of the display window. "Like those shells?" she asks in a voice that demands a positive answer. "I get them from as far away as Australia. Some are from Fiji and the Great Barrier Reef. Even got a shipment today from Greece."

"What do you have to know to run a shell shop?"

"The first thing is a thorough knowledge of the science of conchology."

Yet another specialization—conchology. "That's right," she declares. "Conchology." She angrily rustles the paper and goes back to her reading.

Many portions of the Mississippi in this area are blighted by jerry-built wooden cabins—instant slums, painted in putrid pastels—which are reached from the highway by deeply rutted mud roads. Their fragile shabbiness contrasts sharply with the beauty and might of the river. Every tenth building is adorned by a "Bait for Sale" sign, giving the impression that the local economy is built upon minnows and earthworms. Occasionally there are old homes, set on large plots. They have a well-lived-in look, with front porches and wooden slat swings hanging by thick chains attached to the porch ceilings. There is still something warm and secure about a house with a porch swing.

McGregor, Iowa

Louisiana, Missouri

Near Dubuque, Iowa

Richard O. Bloom lives in such a house, north of Davenport, next to where they are putting in another nuclear power plant. The construction activity generates a huge cloud of white dust which engulfs the whole project and swirls up into the sky. It is clear in the field north of the plant, except for a plume of heavy brown dust that traces the path of Bloom's tractor. He stops at the edge of the field to stretch his long legs.

"I feel a lot of ways toward that river," he says. "It's changed. Polluted. In August the river will be a greenish color. Nobody has the right to do that to the river. After all, a lot of that water is for the humans to drink. We're losing our birds and fish, too." He pauses and kicks open a large clod of dry dirt.

"I've always enjoyed the river . . . up until about December. I lost a boy in it. My boy was six. He and his cousin were out exploring, like all boys that age, like kids do. He was just a little kid. He went out on a shelf of ice. It was the kind of thing that attracts kids. I have five children living, but something like that changes your attitude."

Bloom begins methodically crushing the fragments from the dirt clod. "That is going to change things around here," he says, motioning toward the partly obscured power plant without looking up from the soil. "You get a little dry spell with this kind of land and you lose everything in it. There are a lot of people who worked their lives away for nothing on this land. Maybe that thing is better for us."

For all practical purposes, the riverfront in Davenport is industrial, with flour mills, a sand and gravel installation, parking lots, and railroad cars loaded down with tons of rusty machine turnings. On a warm spring night downtown Davenport was deserted; the parking lot at the river's edge was vacant. Looked at in the moonlight, it became clear that the river had ceased to be a wild, undisciplined beauty hurtling across the countryside. It had become increasingly a convenience for commerce, another tool, a receptacle for sewage, a per-cent per-mile per-pound bargain for shippers, a slimy path for sportsmen in boats heading toward smaller, less violated waters.

Davenport

Route 22, Iowa

Illinois

Iowa

But the Mississippi does not easily surrender its independence. In 1965, during a cataclysm that began with the melting snow high in Minnesota, the river bolted its banks in a major flood. The water spilled into Davenport, turning a minor league baseball stadium at the river's edge into a swamp. "It was a terrible shame," reported a woman in the stands, as the Quad-City Angels played the Quincy Cubs in a night game. "This field wasn't right for the whole season." A devoted fan, she carried in her purse a worn postcard showing the swamped diamond and outfield. It takes the purest of fan devotion to follow teams like the Quad-City Angels. That night's game was a debacle. With seven unearned runs, the Angels won 12 to 3. The only excitement was generated by the men operating the scoreboard, who were always several minutes behind the fumblers on the field. Shrieks of "Fix the god-damned scoreboard!" drowned out the cries of popcorn hawkers roaming the nearly empty stands. The hapless ballplayers had one consolation: the woman with the postcard, her husband, and several other couples were throwing a big cookout that night for the two teams.

Across the river in Rock Island, Illinois, it was prom night for a group of teen-agers gathering at the downtown *YMCA*. The girls, thick boned with precisely arranged hairdos and gowns made at home, were escorted toward the orange school buses by self-conscious young boys in white dinner jackets. The couples moved between a line of parents poised with cameras. Nervous grins gave way to quick flinches as flashbulbs popped. When boarding the bus, the boys were more cautious than the girls, carefully avoiding any surface that might smudge their spotless jackets. Once on the bus, the kids relaxed; the girls rested their heads on the boys' shoulders, and everyone regained assurance in the friendly confines.

Davenport

Rock Island, Illinois

In the next town, Moline, two shapely girls—past, alas, the irrevocable innocence of prom nights and padded gowns—danced on a stand behind the bar of a go-go joint. There were only three men at the bar: a bouncer with a trunklike flashlight used for checking ID's and subduing rowdy customers; a tense, middle-aged man in a three-button suit; and a surly drunk, relentlessly downing drinks called "blacksmith's helpers." "Doesn't anyone in here serve whites?" The drunk scowled, slamming his beer glass on the bar. The bouncer began flicking his flashlight on and off, as though checking the shine on his shoes. The man in the suit grew increasingly fidgety, eyeing the door, perhaps plotting a retreat. One of the girls scrambled down from the dancing perch to draw the man a draft. The other girl, never taking her eyes from a flickering beer sign on the far side of the bar, danced on into the night, oblivious.

South of the Quad Cities, past signs proclaiming the Dye Funeral Home and Weed Park, is the town of Muscatine. Samuel Clemens, who once lived there (the site of his home is now occupied by a filling station), remembered the town's summer sunsets. "I have never seen any, on either side of the ocean, that equaled them. They used the broad, smooth river as a canvas, and painted on it every imaginable dream of color." Families now come from several hundred miles away to rent houseboats in Muscatine. After some cursory lessons, they push off, instant river pilots, to experience the drama of the river.

On one of the high hills that line the Mississippi in this area is the old Musser home, which commands a striking view of the town and a long stretch of the river. It is a typical lumber baron's home: floor-to-ceiling windows on the main floor, pillared wide porches, leaded-glass windows, and elaborate chandeliers within. On the landing between the first and second floor, a stained-glass window throws a spectrum of colors across the steps. It is not difficult to imagine a prosperous lumberman, thumbs thrust into vest pockets, standing proudly on the porch gazing upriver in search of a Mississippi raft. But times have changed. The Musser house is now a makeshift church, with services held in what was apparently the first-floor parlor. An office in downtown Muscatine is rented by social activists assisting Mexican workers imported to pick tomatoes. A few fading building signs hint at the once flourishing pearl button industry. "That is long gone now," a local historian noted. "Plastic buttons are much better anyway."

Muscatine,
Iowa

The Santa Fe Railroad crosses the Mississippi at Fort Madison, over a 3,347-foot-long, twenty-four-span bridge that accommodates trains and cars on its two levels. Cars pay a bridge fee to the Santa Fe. The modern diesels are more swift and powerful than 2913, but the old steam engine of that number, which sits on a short run of track surrounded by a locked fence, is still an impressive image of power and a fit monument to the days when the cry "Boo-ard!" was one of the most romantic sounds in the nation. Those days are long gone. Gone, too, are the days when a workingmen's newspaper could declare: "Turkey for the railroad and buzzard for the toiling and frugal yeomanry; that is the motto of the monopolies." A freight train engineer no longer works from sunup to sundown. He puts in either eight hours or one hundred miles, whichever comes first. If he's on a fast freight, those one hundred miles can come very fast. The Santa Fe's Super C, billed as the world's fastest freight train, makes it between Chicago and Los Angeles in about forty hours—but there are eighteen crew changes en route.

Harry E. Roland and J. W. "Joe" Elliott were in the cab of the Super C as it sped toward the Mississippi and Fort Madison. "My dad was on the railroad," Harry said, "but, you know, I always wanted to fire one of those steam engines. I liked the whistle and the rocking and the rolling and the sound of those damned things. But they could really ride rough. If you ever rode a hayrack over frozen plowed ground, that was it. But there was something about one of those that had it all over diesels." Elliott, whose house in Fort Madison overlooks the Mississippi, feels the same way about trains. He occasionally takes visitors down to the park at the river, where he ends up climbing into Number 2913. "You used to run these by your ear," he said. "You could tell by the sound of the exhaust if you were getting the most from the steam." Roland and Elliott have their own traditions: they don't pay much attention to the river. Samuel Clemens would have frowned on Roland and Elliott; he had little love for the railroad and indeed charged it with "ripping the sacred solitude to rags and tatters with its devil's war whoop and the roar of thunder of its rushing wheels."

Some of the small towns south of Fort Madison, such as New Boston, are shriveling up, disappearing into the earth. The only busy place in New Boston is the filling station.

"Things get pretty active around here in New Boston," the station attendant said.

"When?"

"About ten o'clock on a Saturday night."

A ferry in Canton, Missouri, shuttles back and forth to Illinois on the east bank. "Raise Flag and Sound Horn for Ferry" reads a sign near a building with a high-water marker from the 1965 flood. With a car it is $1.00 one way, $1.50 round trip. Grain costs 1½ cents per bushel. The Canton postmaster and a letter carrier work on the ferry. "It's like any other business," the letter carrier said. "Some days you do better than others." The Canton Chamber of Commerce provides a sticker which allows Illinois residents to use the ferry free on Saturday nights for shopping on the Missouri side. The current is swift, and the ferry operator stays on the alert for tows and pleasure craft. "If you make a good landing on this river you are just a good guesser," he said.

"Don't be so danged retiring," said a chubby old farmer in bib overalls and a tiny, puffy engineer's cap. He had a stubble of beard, and traces of tobacco juice stained his chin.

"Come on up and let me show you Mar," the farmer said. The town of Meyer, north of Canton on the Illinois side, is set behind a tall levee. It is made up of very small wooden homes, well maintained, and shaded by large drooping trees.

"We got just a few people left here in Mar. One, two right in front of you in that house. And then over in that place. Ah, let me count. One, two, three, four, five, six, seven. Old Man Mills and Howie are eight and nine. Medford and his wife. Fry lives back at the corner here. His wife, too. Dab Raider and his brother. Then there's Russ Hemming and Donnie Hemming . . . and, ah, ah, Harold Foster. There's another family in a trailer back there. Well, that's not many at all, is it? There used to be people in Mar. Ain't any more. One farmer used to farm two hundred acres. Now he farms six hundred."

The social center of Meyer is Bud's Let's Go Inn. A sign behind the bar declares: "When you see a boy with a fishing pole, followed by his faithful dog, you can be sure they are not headed for some juvenile court." Another: "Place your orders for smoked turkeys. Will smoke June 2."

The bartender was imposing in size, with pants that hung precariously beneath a drooping belly just barely covered by a badly stretched T-shirt. He was complaining about the rain. It got worse when two women in Levis and men's dress shirts strolled in and bought some night crawlers. They were fussy and complained about the selection. But then a young barefoot boy, his pants held up by suspenders, walked timidly into the inn and went right to the center of the long bar. Without looking up, he fished a handful of coins from his pocket and laid out twenty-five pennies on the bar. The bartender leaned as far over the cooler and bar as his paunch would permit and meticulously counted the pennies.

"Twenty-five pieces of bubble gum, please," the boy said.

Rubbing his hands on the T-shirt, the bartender reached back under the cash register, past a badly scratched leather dice cup and a revolver, and pulled out a box of gum from which he counted out twenty-five pieces.

"Did you earn that money, boy?"

The boy, carefully packing the gum into his pockets, nodded. The bartender threw in a few extra pieces for good measure.

The boy left, heading off toward the levee. "We raise good boys around here," the bartender said. "That boy earned his bubble gum."

If there is one town that has come to symbolize the Mississippi and barefoot boys, it is Hannibal, Missouri. The town is butted up against the river, in fact as in legend. High bluffs and hills, some two hundred feet tall, drop down to the town and the river; across the wide stretch of water, past the mysterious islands that enthralled Huck Finn and Tom Sawyer, is the flatland of Illinois. A Spanish surveyor bestowed the name of Hannibal on a small creek, now known as Bear Creek, which empties into the Mississippi at what is now the town. Samuel Langhorne Clemens was raised in Hannibal at a time when the nation and the world seemed to tie up daily at the main street. The boats that stopped at Hannibal carried circus troups, revivalists, rivermen, planters, journalists, immigrants, drovers, gamblers, painted women—an endless variety of people with endless means and motives. Boys a few miles inland might lead the most provincial of lives, but in Hannibal the river offered a cosmopolitan education.

"When a circus came and went," Clemens recalled, "it left us all burning to become clowns; the first Negro minstrel show that ever came to our section left us all suffering to try that kind of life; now and then we had a hope that, if we lived and were good, God would permit us to be pirates. These ambitions faded out, each in its turn; but the ambition to be a steamboatman always remained."

The cry of "S-t-e-a-m-boat a-coming!" would bring energy and activity to the sleepy towns, and the young boys peered in envy at the man in the glass-and-gingerbread pilothouse perched on the Texas deck. At the age of nine Clemens stole onto a steamboat headed downriver for St. Louis, concealing himself under a lifeboat on the upper deck. The boy could not resist the whistles and bells, the steady threshing of the paddle wheel. After an hour he crept from his cover to look at the passing shore and to feel part of the great ship. He was quickly discovered and put ashore nine miles south of Hannibal at Louisiana. But he would not forget those moments.

After working briefly as a printer on his brother's newspaper in Hannibal, Clemens moved against the westward tide and worked in the back shops of newspapers in New York City and Philadelphia, only to rejoin his brother on a paper in Keokuk, Iowa. A $50 banknote he found on the street there bankrolled him for expeditions to St. Louis and Cincinnati, where he worked as a printer and wrote travel articles which he signed "Thomas Jefferson Snodgrass." From Cincinnati, Clemens set off on the steamboat *Paul Jones* for a trip that would hopefully carry him to another river, the Amazon. The *Paul Jones* rekindled his childhood ambition to be a pilot on the Mississippi. He cajoled the pilot, a testy, foul-tongued man named Horace Bixby, to take him on as an apprentice. Clemens eventually paid $400 for seventeen months of training, without which, as he later noted, he "would have drifted into the ministry, the penitentiary, or a graveyard somewhere." Bixby was not a tolerant tutor, and Clemens, who complained his "memory was never loaded with anything but blank cartridges," took his training seriously.

"My boy," Bixby told him, "you must get a little memorandum book; and every time I tell you a thing, put it down right away. There's only one way to be a pilot, and that is to get this entire river by heart. You have to know it just like A-B-C."

Having learned the intricacies of piloting a treacherous river by memory and instinct, and of finding his way in the dark obscure plantation landings, Twain was licensed as a pilot. He first set out as a cub on the dismal packet *John J. Roe,* a decrepit boat which rivermen claimed could run all day in the shade of a big tree. "The only races on the *Roe,"* Clemens recalled, "were with rafts and islands." Clemens worked as pilot until 1861, when the Civil War disrupted river traffic. From the Mississippi he was off to the silver mines of Nevada and the gold mines of California—newspapering, traveling, and writing. As he later put it: "I became a scribbler of books, and an immovable fixture among the other rocks of New England." As a writer, of course, he turned back to the little river town of Hannibal for his most enduring works. "All that goes to make the me in me," he said, "was in a Missouri village on the other side of the globe."

Now the state's fourth industrial center, Hannibal is a town of approximately twenty thousand. It is quiet and somewhat smug about its world wide reputation. It has placed bronze statues of Huck and Tom at the foot of Cardiff Hill, where the two shared many exploits. A lighthouse at the top of the hill has taken the place of a house where a lantern was kept in the window to guide river pilots. A statue of Samuel Clemens, facing toward the mile-wide Mississippi, stands on one of the bluffs in a city park.

Clemens was raised in a two-story, white frame house with green trim at 208 Hill Street. It is just off the main street, only a short stroll from the river. Built in 1844, the house now seems to lean precariously toward the river, and the floors and stairs have an unsettling sag. "You could never get a mortgage on this one," said a tourist as he prowled through the house, which is filled with furniture and bric-a-brac from the 1840's. Next door is a museum containing a fantastic variety of Mark Twain mementos, ranging from the table on which he wrote *Tom Sawyer* to his orchestrelle, a bizzarre musical instrument, half player-piano, half organ.

With the home and the museum illustrating the sharp contrast between his humble beginning and the success he enjoyed as a great author, one begins to get a surer sense of Samuel Clemens. Reared at a unique time and place in American history, he later used his natural literary genius to resurrect those circumstances with a truth and beauty that still defy age and imitation. But those qualities now exist only in the pages of his books. Hannibal, inevitably, justifiably, has changed. In the main, it is now a town of small modern businesses, along with a gaudy settlement of antique shops and enterprises that draw their livelihood off legends. Across the street from the Clemens house and museum is a gift shop where for 69 cents one can buy a tacky cup inscribed with the Lord's Prayer. Uphill is the Mark Twain Drive-In Restaurant, which through a prominently displayed sign implores its customers to "Please Show Courtesy." And Clemens, who so deftly recorded the harshness one man could feel for another, would have understood the traditional meaning of another, more foreboding sign: "We reserve the right to park and serve our customers."

"I can't tell you how many tourists come here," said a woman who runs a trinket shop near the museum. "They come in cars and trailers, a lot of big families. They don't dress as formal as they used to. They are happy-go-lucky types, though some of the men tend to look a bit irritated. Looks like some of them would rather spend their vacations at home than out on the road with squawking kids. But most are polite. Some of the little devils you have to look out for, though. They steal. Not many of them, but enough. If a big bus filled with kids pulls in, it is really something. We're all on the alert."

The woman feels the river town needs something new and startling to boost the tourist trade. "Some men in Illinois want to come down here and put in a wax museum with all kinds of those Twain characters and stuff. I think that's a good idea. Don't you?"

Hannibal's downtown streets are wide, and in the town square, surrounded by green park benches, is a priceless relic of mid-America—a bandstand. An elderly man was sound asleep on a park bench, in spite of the raucous blare of a rock-'n-roll record. The sounds came from loudspeakers attached to a one-room shack stuck at the top of steel scaffolding at one corner of the park. Robert Eugene Usherwood, living about three stories up in his wood cell, was sitting on a narrow porch, twisting his radio dial from one station to another. "I'm trying to do something for Hannibal by setting the record for tower sitting," he shouted down to incredulous tourists. "I'm also the champion barrel stomper. I can stomp more paper into a barrel than anyone in the world. It takes a lot of practice and strong leg muscles and everything else." As the tourists turned to walk away he looked hurt. One of them, a woman, glanced over her shoulder at Usherwood, who was already back at his radio, filling the park with a screeching blare as he spun the dial.

The boys down the street in Schaffer's Smoke House were intent on their pinochle game, uninterested in any tower-sitting record. Schaffer's hasn't changed over the years. It is dark and cool in the narrow store. The walls are lined with embossed tin squares; the showcases in the front room, filled mostly with conventional cigarettes, also house exotic and obscure brands of cigars and chewing tobacco. The store does a brisk trade in snuff. A single bright lamp hangs from the ceiling of the rear room, illuminating a round card table. The atmosphere is definitely masculine. A wall is adorned with calendars and old pictures; one group shows the late House Speaker and Missouri Congressman, Champ Clark, at a Shriner's outing in 1920.

"The smoke shop has been this way since the nineties," Schaffer said. "If it was good enough for Mark Twain, I see no sense in changing it just to be changing. Twain was first here about 1902. He came into town to make an address and just dropped by to relax and play a few hands."

At one time there was a cigar factory next door to the smoke shop. Long abandoned but in some circles fondly remembered brands, such as Rabbit's Foot, Harmony, Old Fisherman, Red Seal, and Missouri Lad, were produced next door.

Hannibal, Missouri [and facing page]

"At one time Hannibal was one of the large cigar-making and shipping centers," Schaffer recalled, drawing leisurely on a darkened corncob pipe. "This was known as the stogie city. My father developed the first Red Seal cigar. Things haven't changed here much, as I see it. I'm here seven days a week. We're open from 6 A.M. to 9 P.M. and there's usually a game. If I ain't loafing here I'm loafing somewhere else.

"This place goes way back and I have a lot in common with it. We've been playing cards in here all those years with no trouble. It is a nice loafing place for salesmen or somebody with an angry wife. You need a place like this. Where you can walk out of your house or your hotel room and find some congenial company and a good honest game. It's twenty cents a game here. Can't get hurt."

Down at the river a little paddle-wheel tourist boat was loading for a trip up and down the Mississippi. The captain was a solidly built river veteran named Arthur Bull. He mingled easily with the families and schoolteachers and teen-agers who turned out for the trip.

"My daddy was captain of an old steamer," said Bull, who was now fifty. "All the kids read *Huck Finn* in my day. At six or seven I'd swim the river and play on the barges. When I was nine my brother and I came down the river on a canoe. We paid one dollar for the canoe. I'd never allow my children to do such things. But in those days it was the depression and there weren't any kids as we know them. Every kid did a man's job, even working as a deck hand.

"Like every kid on the river, I dreamed of having a boat. Now I got a bus line, some real estate, and we'll soon have four of these tourist boats. That's the river for you. It's the only place in the world where a guy without education can make $12,000 to $15,000 a year after four or five years." Bull got his grubstake through an unusual source—wrestling. "I saw this man in a carnival hold up a $5 bill and say the man who could take his man could have the $5. 'Come and get it,' he said. I went and got it. I had seen some scuffling around on the river, and from then I wrestled on and off. If I needed to make some money to meet a payroll or something, I'd go back to wrestling. Everybody needs that initial scratch to get going. I got mine from wrestling.

"But I always come back to this river. The real people have the river."

The little stern-wheeler sightseeing boat churns through the dark opaque water as Bull regales the tourists with tales of great riverboat pilots and his own experiences on the tows. He also points out islands and landmarks featured in the Twain books. "Up there in that hill is the cave where Injun Joe died and where Tom and Becky were lost." They take tours through the cave today, along a precise route marked by bleak light bulbs hanging from the ceiling. It's cold in the cave, 52 degrees, and the guide uses a strong lamp to point out Indian markings on the ceiling and directional signs left on the walls by early explorers. There are also jutting rocks which, if illuminated from the correct angle and aided by an expansive imagination, resemble battleships, Injun Joe, spider monkeys, and Winston Churchill. There is also a deep recess along one wall where Jesse James and his gang allegedly took refuge from the elements and posses. At the entrance to the cave, however, is a stark sign, jerking one's attention away from Jesse James and Becky Thatcher and primitive Indians. "Fallout Shelter. Capacity 3,000."

Outside Hannibal, startled motorists slowed their cars to gaze in amazement at a bored, somewhat arrogant-looking camel under a clump of trees in a field of knee-high grass. Farther back in the field were nine elephants, ripping huge patches of green from the earth and, with a quick downward snap of their trunks, hurling them into their mouths. Though tents weren't up it was circus day in Hannibal, and the animals had arrived before the other elements of the over-the-road Carson and Barnes Circus. A few house trailers were already crowded under trees that, hopefully, would provide relief from the heat. A heavy-set man was lounging near his front door, listening to jazz on a portable stereo. His children were playing next door and his wife was inside fixing a meal. They were citizens of a mobile city of badly stained canvas and miles of hemp and thick snakes of electrical wire that each morning arose to an archaic kind of greatness, throve in the blare and the bizarrerie of its own making, and was then broken down to be put up again elsewhere.

Circus, Hannibal [and following pages]

"Hannibal's just another town to us," a circus hand said. "They all look alike from the highway. One day one town, one day the next—you can't even keep up with the names. They don't change much, except in one town the catsup may cost more than in the next. God damn the Lions Club in this place. They were supposed to cut the god-damned grass." He slapped the side of a low-slung tank trailer truck with his worn cane. The blow didn't phase the truck's occupant, "Goliath, the Blood-Sweating Hippopotamus from the River Nile." Stilled by lethargy and years of confinement, Goliath was a stationary hulk in a pool of water so black that in comparison the Mississippi seemed crystal clear. With the arrival of more trucks and cars and trailers, the circus city began to take form. The elephants were herded from their vast open table of land to help erect the main tent. "Move it up, move it up," shouted the mahouts, urging the beasts to pull up the support poles. A roustabout slapped the broad flank of an elephant with a stick, which raised a dense puff of dust. The field, once silent, resounded with the clank of sledgehammers pounding metal stakes.

"It's good to see a circus come up in an open field," said a Missouri resident who turned out to watch the spectacle. "I can't take to a circus in an auditorium. I started with a circus once, back when I was a kid, with Clyde Beatty. Now *there* was a man who could train animals. As a boy he was always training cats and dogs and chickens. When Clyde first went off to the circus he used my dog in his act. I went along to help look after him. Spot was his name, just a plain fox terrier. But Clyde had that dog trained so he could do anything but talk. I really liked the circus but I went on to school. I'm an accountant now." From his admiring look at the animals and the workers, one got the impression that occasionally, perhaps, when blinded by the unending blur of debits and credits, he might muse about what would have happened to his life if he had stayed with the circus, if he had turned in the adding machine for a ticket booth and his sedate family Chevrolet for a silver house trailer that carried the dust of every state in the nation.

The crowd arrived for the matinee. No boys in bare feet and straw hats attempted to sneak under a tent. Instead they arrived with their mothers in air-conditioned cars. The circus was cleverly laid out, so that to reach the main tent the crowd had to pass through a funnel of displays and exhibits and three-balls-for-a-quarter, everybody-gets-a-prize games. There was only one possible detour —through the sideshow, which featured a sword swallower, a tattooed man, and other curiosities. A group of grade-school children watched the sword swallower give his blade a cursory wipe with a handkerchief, then drop the gleaming steel down his throat. No applause. The kids weren't impressed. In a week during 1969 they had watched three men walk on the moon. A sword swallower was pretty tame stuff in the days of Apollo. The tattooed man fared no better. "Yes, folks, they do call me the tattooed man. You can see that when I take off my cape I do have quite a few tattoos. Don't be bashful. I only have twenty thousand." The kids ignored the tattoos and instead looked into the eyes of this man; they seemed more concerned with his meaning than his plumage.

Most of the onlookers moved without comment to the next display, not bothering to pay a quarter to see a dwarf cow the tattooed man kept concealed in a box at the rear of his stage. "It's not the fastest audience I've ever had," the tattooed man said, brushing his shoulder-length red hair away from his face. His body was a grotesquerie of red, blue, and purple drawings. People, he said, generally seemed more interested in the "why" of the tattoos than in the decorations themselves. "It isn't polite to tell them about this. I apologize for even saying it to you, but I hate people. I hate people so much I went and had myself tortured. I felt each and every tattoo; it hurt. Those who say it doesn't hurt must have been drunk when it was done. I like traveling with the circus because of the highways. Traveling over the highways, I don't think much about people. I don't see many." The few people who lingered behind to hear this explanation quickly walked away, depressed by the man and his story. The tattooed man was left alone with his dwarf cow and a shabby robe he used to cover his tortured body.

The circus was good—a bright and rapidly paced celebration of an old art form. The audience was joyous, the performers seemed very beautiful. It wasn't until she was outside the tent that one noticed that the woman on the lead elephant had sagging jowls and chubby, vein-scarred legs.

An arm of stone palisades escorts the river on its east bank as it flows down toward St. Louis. The lock and dam at Alton, Illinois, backs the river into a scenic lake which, during the summer, attracts pleasure crafts that dart about the stodgy tows and tugboats. The river is also dotted with blinds used by duck hunters, and small cabins rise from stilts on islands close to the shore. The Illinois River joins the Mississippi above Alton, a town perched on rolling hills overlooking the big river. Alton has a distinctive history. It is graced with brick streets and sedate old mansions topped by widow's walks. At the waterfront is a plaque commemorating the site as the scene of a Lincoln-Douglas debate, and nearby is a statue of a World War I American doughboy. A few miles downriver is a small park which marks the launching place of the Lewis and Clark expedition, the journey from the Mississippi up the Missouri and across the Rockies to the Pacific Ocean.

Shortly after the turn of the nineteenth century, President Thomas Jefferson grew increasingly anxious for exploration of the vast openness west of the Mississippi, which left a frustrating void on his maps. He commissioned two army officers, William Clark and Meriwether Lewis, to carry the flag west. The "Corps of Discovery," as the expedition was called, wintered in 1893–1894 on the Illinois side of the Mississippi, at its point of confluence with the Missouri River. Clark stood on the small spit of land and looked across at the river that would carry him into a wilderness never before visited by white men. He noted in his journal that "the Missouri which mouths immediately opposite me is the river we intend ascending as soon as the weather will permit." On Sunday, May 13, 1804, Clark started off for the Pacific. "I set out at 4 o'clock P.M.," he noted, "in the presence of many of the neighbouring inhabitents, and proceeded on under a jentle brease up the Missourie." The expedition traveled in three vessels, the largest of which was a twenty-two-oar keelboat which also carried a square sail. A few miles upriver the expedition met Lewis, who had moved ahead "to fix off the Osage chiefs." The unified party then plunged into a land as distant and remote and potentially dangerous as outer space is to the explorers of the twentieth century.

On November 15 of the following year, the group reached the mouth of the Columbia River, completing a four-thousand-mile trek, the first crossing north of Mexico to the Pacific Ocean. Clark's journal entry upon reaching what he presumed to be the ocean reflected the quiet thankfulness of a man who had just completed a journey of hardship and peril: "Ocean in view! O! the joy." The expedition produced valuable scientific observations and collections, but, more important, the Americans had thrust west and there was now a slash across the void on the maps. The way had been broken for the expansion of a nation. The expedition—which suffered only one death and one desertion over the entire route—returned to St. Louis on September 23, 1806. "They really have the appearance of Robinson Crusoes—dressed entirely in buckskins," a resident of the village noted. The citizenry turned out to welcome the heroes: "the people gathered on the shore and hizzared three cheers."

Lewis became governor of the northern part of the Louisiana Territory. Clark was initially named governor of Missouri, then served as superintendent of Indian affairs in St. Louis until his death in 1838. He was buried on Meadow Lane in St. Louis' Bellefontaine Cemetery, overlooking the infamous Chain of Rocks in the Mississippi. His grave is marked by a bronze bust and a tall granite obelisk. It has a pertinent inscription: "Behold, the Lord thy God hath set the land before thee, go up and possess it." A good deal of the history of St. Louis, and of the Mississippi, is represented in that cemetery.

While the cemetery and its ornate markers (the monument at the grave of Captain Isaiah Sellers depicts a pilot with a river map at the helmsman's wheel) represent the past, one can look downriver and see a silver rainbow soaring over the downtown waterfront area. It is the Gateway Arch, a stainless steel catenary arch designed by Eero Saarinen which commemorates Jefferson's Louisiana Purchase and the expansion west through the river town of St. Louis. The Gateway Arch, the nation's tallest monument, has sparked a dramatic renaissance along the waterfront, which now houses office buildings, apartment complexes, motels, a fifty-thousand-seat sports stadium, and the Spanish Pavilion building imported from the New York World's Fair. But the arch, which eventually will be complemented by a park development about the base and an underground museum, dominates the area, compelling the eye to follow the gentle curves until they marry 630 feet in the air. Visitors can ride to the top of the monument in little capsule cars, which make little jerking adjustments to the shape of the arch as they rise. The view is spectacular.

St. Louis [and facing page]

The arch stands near a village site selected in 1763 by the French fur trader Pierre Laclède Ligueste. Fourteen miles south of the mouth of the Missouri River, the village was named after Louis XV. The shadow of the arch marks what emerged as the commercial center for the development of the West. Mountain men and Indian tribes shipped mounds of pelts to the thriving St. Louis fur market. One of the buildings cleared for the Gateway development was the old stone depot of Manuel Lisa, who made thirteen journeys up the muddy Missouri to gather furs. He built the first St. Louis trading post in the West, in Crow country, at the mouth of the Big Horn River. During the summer of a good fur season, the stench from piles of pelts outside his warehouse permeated the waterfront. Riverboats were then a constant presence, bringing men and merchandise from the North, South, and East. St. Louis produced wagons for the Santa Fe trail, plows to rip into the soil of the plains, dragoon saddles, rifles, and cast-iron stoves for baking bread or holding at bay the biting wind that swept down from the mountains.

One writer left a vivid description of those who began the trek west in the lower decks of the riverboats: "All sorts of men and women, of all trades, from all parts of the world, of all possible manners and habits. There is the half-horse and half-alligator Kentucky flat-boatman, swaggering and boasting of his prowess, his rifle, and his wife. One is sawing away on his wretched old fiddle all day long; another is grinding a knife or razor; here is a party playing cards; and in yonder corner is a dance to the sound of a jew's harp; whilst few are trying to demean themselves soberly, by sitting in silence or reading a book. But it is almost impossible— the wondrous tale and horrible Indian story they are telling; the bottle and jug are freely circulating; and the boisterous and deafening laugh is incessantly raised, sufficient to banish every vestige of seriousness, thought and sense. Amidst this confusion, and even in the minds of those lank and laconic men who sat astride piles of freight leaning their chins forward on long, bony, calloused hands, there worked the silent factor of the great American dream . . . everybody . . . dreamed of the rich lands to the West."

North of the Gateway Arch is the last stand of old buildings with a distinct waterfront atmosphere. The streets are narrow, and the brick buildings rise four or five stories, with tall, narrow windows, many of them decorated with barely legible signs that recall past days of prosperity. The area conveys the impression of a Sunday afternoon in the 1880's, with the citizenry off on a picnic, downing German Thuringer sausage and beer from the Anheuser-Busch brewery.

The area north of the arch is now mainly dominated by pigeons, who proudly strut on the windowsills, in and out of the rusted bars covering ground- and second-floor windows. At the moment, there are elaborate plans to develop this neighborhood, known as Laclede's Landing, into a tourist and residential area similar to Ghirardelli Square in San Francisco or the French Quarter in New Orleans. Promoters feel that visitors will flock to Laclede's Landing, if for no other reason than that only five thousand of the twenty thousand people who daily visit the Gateway Arch during tourist season can reach the observation deck at the top because of the limited transportation system.

St. Louis abounds in historical significance contrasted with signs of modern enterprise. The city has a distinct feeling of vitality; one senses a community struggling at least to keep abreast of the urban problems of the moment while at the same time attempting to preserve its past. There is little unanimity as to what constitutes the best balance between past and present. Some social activists consider the Laclede's Landing project a tragic municipal folly—a waste of effort and resources that could better be applied to eradicating extensive slums and other social problems. Others feel that, linked to the Gateway development, Laclede's Landing would provide an immediate transition from the past to the present, so that in a few blocks one could traverse more than a century in the history of a unique town.

A little village about sixty miles south of St. Louis which missed the acceleration of twentieth-century modernity and exists today as a picture-book version of a more quaint America is St. Genevieve. Founded by the French before 1735, it has more than twenty buildings between 150 and 200 years old. Although practically pampered with care, these buildings sit naturally in a placid community where life moves at a slow measured pace.

Most of the old homes are open to visitors. The early St. Genevieve houses were modeled after those in Quebec and Normandy, but the sultry summers along the Mississippi prompted the addition of "galleries," wide-open porches which extend around all four sides of the houses.

"If you like old houses you have to visit this town," Mrs. Mildred R. Baum said as she mixed a prescription behind the pharmacist's window in the Rutledge drugstore. "There are a lot of new families in this town, a lot of old families too. But no snobbishness. The people who could be snobbish, or should be, were never that way." A slight, spry woman with white hair, she moved out into the cluttered little drugstore. "My father was a doctor here. In the palmy days this town had four doctors—Dr. Lanning, Dr. Hench, Dr. Meyer, and Pop, Dr. Rutledge, my father. You see, each doctor then had his own drugstore."

Mrs. Baum has ushered the drugstore, which was founded about 1902, into the 1970's, and to mark the progress she has decorated the store with pictures from the old days. One old picture shows a group of mustachioed men standing in the street, with picks and shovels and wheelbarrows. "The men in town donated a day to fixing the main street. See those ones down front? The politicians and businessmen. They didn't lift a finger. The only work they did that day was to have their pictures taken. Things don't change."

Mrs. Baum is also irate over attempts to control the Mississippi, which she thinks are miserable flops. "Now you look at this picture. It was taken next to a walnut tree up on the hill. See, you can see the river. It was about a quarter of a mile away. Now you can't even see the river from that hill. It is more than a mile away. It's due to industrial and government bumbling. The river is so narrowed down to nothing that any time anybody spits in it, it floods."

The former residents of Kaskaskia, Illinois, were they still around, would doubtless have differed with Mrs. Baum about efforts to control the Mississippi. The town, founded in the early 1700's before the French came to New Orleans, thrived within the V formed by the merger of the Kaskaskia and Mississippi rivers. Recognizing the town's potential, Louis XV presented the citizens with a 650-pound bell, cast in 1741, which around its upper rim bears the legend: "For the Church of Illinois, with the compliments of the King from beyond the sea."

The town was on the Kaskaskia River, two miles east of the Mississippi. The first major omen came in 1844, when a flood sent eight feet of water into the town. The Mississippi began to eat away at its own east bank, and by 1881 was within four hundred feet of Kaskaskia. The river was a writhing python, strangling the once-promising town. The residents fled, and over the years their homes and stores simply dropped into the river. As late as 1906 one could see a chimney remaining, but by 1915 the town was in the center of the Mississippi channel. Old-timers recall rowing on the river and looking down at the murky shadows of the buildings that once constituted the first capital city of the state of Illinois.

On the Illinois side of the Mississippi is the town of Chester, which is recalled in river lore for a series of unscheduled stops visited upon the community during the flood of 1844 by the steamboat *Belle Air*. The river was then well over its banks, and the *Belle Air,* following a common procedure in such circumstances, took shortcuts by cutting across country. The pilot of the *Belle Air,* however, having miscalculated, found himself steaming down one of Chester's main streets. The steamboat proceeded to slam into a three-story building, toppling the third floor into the water. From there it rammed a four-story stone mill, ricocheted off other buildings, and destroyed the local jail before making it from main street to mainstream.

Chester is best known today as the site of a major state prison. It sits down near the river, a heavy stone building, squat and bleak, as desolate as the lives of those confined within. On the hills above the prison, overlooking the river, trusties work in the fields and along the highways. They tend to keep their eyes on their work, perhaps out of embarrassment, perhaps because they are afraid to look too closely at the freedom represented by the Mississippi and the roads.

Downriver is Grand Tower, pronounced Grand Tar by the natives, which Twain noted in *Life on the Mississippi* as "a busier place than it had been in old times, but it seemed to need some repairs here and there, and a new coat of whitewash all over." It still needs repairs and whitewash, though the tower, a massive pillar of rock capped by a stand of trees, still stands majestically on a quarter-acre island on the Missouri side of the river. At one time the town had a population of 3,500. "I would say that Grand Tar today has 850 people and four churches," said a local merchant. "It's not crowded, and it's a fine place to live."

On the west side of the levee that protects Grand Tower from the river, a Coast Guard vessel had pulled in to repair a navigational marker bowled over in high water by floating timber. Coast Guardsman Lou Lozano was directing his work force across the soggy brown muck, through flights of large determined mosquitoes. "Damn, I miss the ocean," said Lozano as his men began putting up a marker indicating that the distance to Cairo, Illinois, was 79.5 miles. "I just can't get used to a river, even this big one. You know, land on both sides of you. I need an ocean, land on one side and saltwater on the other."

Downriver at Thebes, the people are very close to the river. The town came to life in the early 1800's as Spar Hawk's Landing, so named because the Sparhawk brothers established a landing there to ship poplar they cut downriver to New Orleans for furniture production. Thebes eventually developed into the county seat, and in 1848 the citizens put the final touches on a courthouse made from unhewn sandstone. The county seat has since been shifted to Cairo, but the courthouse stands on the hill overlooking the town and the Mississippi, a lonely sentinel from another century.

"The state wants to tear down this building and just put up a historical marker," said a woman dusting books in the main first-floor room of the old courthouse. The room is filled with mannequins costumed in frocks from the steamboat days, along with posters, collections of photographs, and antique tools. The only shiny thing in the room is a soft-drink machine. Beneath the main floor is a dungeon, separated into two dark rooms with narrow windows crossed by steel bars. "This was the only town on the Illinois side of the river that had a dungeon," the woman explained as she led visitors through the rooms. "One room was for men, the other for women. Far as we can tell, this is where Dred Scott was imprisoned for a while. The history books say he was kept in a dungeon in lower Illinois, and this was the only dungeon in these parts. Can you imagine standing behind one of these windows and looking down at the boats moving upriver toward freedom? That must have hurt." The woman shivered, drew her sweater tighter around her shoulders, and moved out into the sun. "We're trying to get industry to move in here so we can save the town and the courthouse. I wish the town would just come back to give the young people a chance. In a town like this, no young boy wants to stay. He'll go to Cape Girardeau or Cairo to make his way, and where will that leave Thebes, without any youngsters?"

It would be difficult to imagine Thebes dropping any further into obscurity. It is already a town of abandoned homes and basements. The end came in the depression, and the symbol of the town's death was the closing of its bank in 1933. Thebes is today virtually deserted. Three old farmers stood in the shade of a vacant gas station and talked to a fourth man sitting on a tractor. Downtown, across from what used to be a train depot and hotel, is a bar. Three teen-age girls in sunfrocks were playing outside, tossing a large plastic ball back and forth. Inside, the bartender was chatting with his nephew, who was soon to graduate from high school, after which he planned to join the Air Force. The uncle was chiding the boy for teasing the giggling girls, who obviously relished the attention.

"What do you whistle at those girls for?" the man asked.

"It's just my nature," the boy answered.

"That isn't polite." The boy grinned at his uncle's displeasure, not out of insolence but more in amusement at the man's lack of understanding.

"Here, take this," the man said with a false gruffness, slapping a ten-dollar bill into the boy's hand. "Go have a good time before the armed forces get you and burn away all that steam." The boy said thanks and went out to join the girls. Their laughter was the only noise in Thebes.

Traveling south from Thebes, toward Cairo, Illinois, one begins to sense an increasing Southern atmosphere. The signs provide hints: "Watermelons for Sale." "Pecans for Sale." "Cairo Cotton Mill." Although in Illinois, Cairo, protected by imposing levees from the merging of the Ohio and Mississippi rivers, is farther south geographically than Richmond, Virginia. In both appearance and attitudes it has far more in common with Arkansas than with Chicago, or for that matter most of the rest of Illinois. This southern portion of the state is known as Little Egypt. One legend has it that early settlers found the area reminiscent of the River Nile. Others claim that hard-pressed frontier families in central and northern Illinois fled south toward the fertile river lands, much as the Israelites moved into Egypt.

Its merging with the Ohio marks a distinct change in the character of the Mississippi. The relatively clear water of the Ohio surrenders meekly to the dominant strength of the brownish yellow waters of the Mississippi. Gone now is any hint of tranquillity, of softness, of the beauty associated with swiftly moving blue along shores of tall green trees. The upper river, born in the austere majesty of northern Minnesota, cut through the countryside a comparatively well-mannered stream moving between cliffs and hills that underscore the drama of the waterway. Strengthened by the Missouri, emboldened by the conquest of the Ohio, the Mississippi now grows rambunctious, surly, even intimidating. It cuts and swerves without warning, constantly changing the countryside as it goes. The upper river may make adjustments in the landscape, but the lower river can ravage it. As Twain said, "The Mississippi is a just and equitable river; it never tumbles one man's farm overboard without building a new farm just like it for that man's neighbor."

Those who settle in the Mississippi's sphere must live and work behind the levees, which run for approximately 3,500 miles along the river and its related streams. The cement and earthen walls range from thirty to fifty feet in height, and the city of New Orleans, which is normally four to seven feet below water level, can fall a full twenty feet below water level during the floods.

From the beginning, the Little Egypt area and the merging of the two rivers had had a bad press from explorers and travelers. In 1796, Andrew Ellicott set out with instructions from President George Washington to determine boundaries in the Lower Mississippi area between the territories of Spain and those of the American Republic. He found the conflux of the two rivers to be, at best, a disappointment. "Those who are descending the Ohio and Mississippi and have been pleased with the prospect of large rivers, rushing together among hills and mountains, will anticipate the pleasure of viewing the conflux of these stupendous waters. But their expectations will not be realized; the prospect is neither grand nor romantic; here are no hills to variegate the scene, no mountains from whose summits the meanderings of the waters may be traced, no chasms through which they have forced their way."

Cairo, Illinois [and following pages]

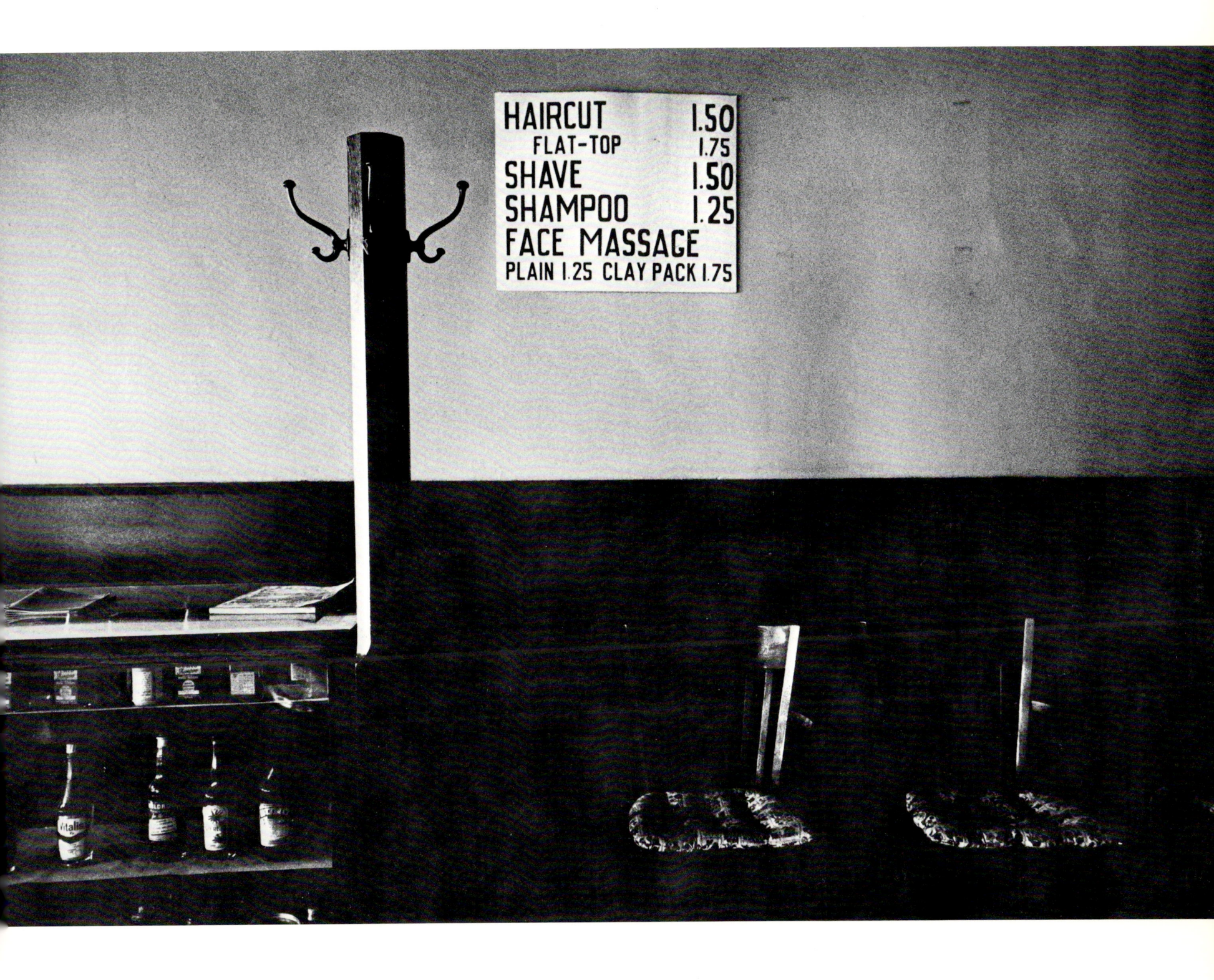

New Madrid, Missouri

Cairo was settled in the late 1830's by Darius B. Holbrook, a New Englander who hired workmen to erect a levee, houses, and stores. But the London firm supporting and publicizing Cairo as a glorious city of the future itself collapsed in 1840. The dream of Cairo died early. The English novelist Charles Dickens, one of many foreigners who had been lured into investing in the futile dream, was particularly bitter. Traveling through the area in 1842, he wrote of the "hateful Mississippi pouring its muddy flood past dismal Cairo . . . a breeding place of fever, augue and death." He reserved further spite for the town for his novel *Martin Chuzzlewit,* in which Cairo provided the actual setting for the vile community of Eden. Equally unimpressed was Herman Melville. In *The Confidence Man,* he noted that "at Cairo the old firm of Fever & Ague is still setting up its unfinished business . . . in the dank twilight fanned with mosquitoes and sparkling with fireflies, the boat now lies before Cairo—that swamp and squalid domain."

There have been a few minor booms through the years, but by 1970 Cairo was in the main a frail community filled with suspicion. Between 1940 and 1965 the population slumped from 14,407 to an estimated 8,500. Jobs disappeared. Plants left. One major employer modernized its facility, in the process diminishing its work force while increasing production. The railroad closed out a roundhouse which once serviced twelve locomotives a day. One of the town's two cotton gins shut down; so did a big cottonseed-oil plant. Alexander County, of which Cairo is the county seat, and neighboring Pulaski County suffered a 20 per cent welfare ratio—the highest in the state. Young people took to reading classified sections of out-of-town newspapers.

"I'm not going to get depressed about this town," a Cairo community leader said. "We are at a very strategic place. I view the Mississippi and the Ohio rivers as great natural resources for Cairo. We are at the hub." Like other community boosters, he claims that more freight tonnage passes Cairo than is handled by any port in the world. But the key word in that claim is not tonnage but *passes*. Union regulations and mechanical capability have discouraged stops at such towns as Cairo, and one can lean against the cement levee wall that protects the downtown and watch the long strings of towboats gliding past Cairo.

But far more demoralizing than the commercial atrophy, and potentially much more damaging, is the blatant hatred between blacks and whites in Cairo. Around 1968 a group of militant blacks arose in Cairo to make demands upon the white leadership. An impasse immediately developed, followed by arson, gunfights, and community chaos. Cairo divided into two armed camps. The blacks boycotted the downtown merchants, and many people switched their allegiance to other, less tense communities.

On a mild spring afternoon, merchants stood in their doorways, idly viewing the few cars and pedestrians in sight. Along with more than thirty empty store fronts in one twelve-block stretch, the scarcity of shoppers gave the town a tragically desperate appearance. A traveling salesman, using his foot to prod a sample case mounted on casters toward his car, paused for a few last words with a merchant. It was obvious the salesman had not received an order.

"You got some real bad feeling in this town," the salesman said. There was compassion in his voice, but also a hint of relief that he was getting out of Cairo.

"Yeh, . . . why don't you put one of our nigras in that case of yours and take him home?"

"We don't need any more colored in my town," the salesman responded.

At the corner a group of young boys were window-shopping on the way home from school. They paused in front of a bank construction site, where the Baptist Youth Fund had decorated the wooden fence along the sidewalk with slogans such as "Let God Put You in the Driver's Seat" and "Snoopy Goes to Church." The boys were polite but angry.

"You better write something good about Cairo."

"Why?"

"Everybody else writes something bad. If you write something good about Cairo it will sell and you'll make a lot of money."

"Why will it sell?"

"Because it will be unique, that's why."

"I don't care what anybody says about this place," said another boy, who couldn't have been more than twelve. "I'm getting out."

"That's not a good way to feel about your home town, particularly if it has some problems."

"They're not my problems. The niggers are taking over here. I don't want to live with them."

The boys strolled down the street, passing under a movie marquee which billed the current attraction: "Clark Gable in Gone with the Wind."

Below Cairo the Mississippi clearly asserts its strength, drawn from thirty-one states, all the way from Montana and western Canada to New York. Now ranging from one-half mile to a mile and a half in width and from fifty to one hundred feet in depth, it becomes an immense physical entity, sending off many smaller entities of its own—surging eddies, capricious currents, sudden boilings. It moves without pattern, looping and curving, but always gnawing at the shore, as if anxious to break free of the restrictions imposed by modern engineering. In many places it is virtually impossible to reach the river, even on the water side of the levee, where it is protected by tree-dotted fields of mud, or bayous, or meandering streams which, in flood season, accept the river and usher it up against the levees.

New Madrid—frequently pronounced New Mad Rid—is on the Missouri side of the Mississippi, at the top of a loop in the river. It is a representative river town—slow, congenial, quick to recall the past, and apprehensive about the present. The barbershop has three chairs, but one is used for stacking newspapers. "There used to be more people here than we could serve," the barber said. "But I don't need but one helper now. The trouble with small towns is that they don't pay union wages. That and modern machinery have moved people out of this country.

New Madrid

"The older people haven't changed," he continued. "The younger people have. They don't want to stay in the small towns. We don't even have a barbers' union. A lot of the young men I worked on when they were smaller now report back to me that they would like to come home. They would rather live here than in the cities. But they can't make any money here. Well, then, let me ask you. Who's gonna keep a nice little town like this up? You know, you and me, we made this country great. With work, sweat, and taxation, we did. Who's gonna keep it up?"

With no ready answer to that question, the barber switched to the old days, recalling the river steamers. "We had a gang of them calling here. They carried livestock, cotton, hogs. That was quite a sight down there. I even saw the nigras load bulls on those steamers. And that was no easy chore. We had some fine nigras on the waterfront here. When they weren't at it, they played cards. That's how we knew them. Dirty Deuces. Ace of Hearts. Ace of Spades. Even all the young niggers are leaving here too." The barber pulled a newspaper from his third chair and sat down to read.

It was crowded in New Madrid that day. With people on the street, and shiny aluminum fronting on some of the buildings, New Madrid appeared prosperous. The library, just off the main street, has records to chart the town's development. Settled in 1788, New Madrid was for many years the only real village between Louisville and Natchez. Under the library flagpole and next to a memorial for Thomas F. Hunter, Jr., who died at the age of twenty on Okinawa, is a cannonball from a major Civil War battle outside New Madrid. The Union troops outmaneuvered the Confederacy during the spring of 1862 and after considerable fighting took seven thousand prisoners.

But the major event in New Madrid's history occurred during the early morning hours of December 16, 1811, when a sudden rumbling of the earth developed into massive convulsions. Roughhewn houses crumbled, burying their occupants in the rubble. Trees tumbled to the ground. Long portions of riverbank crumbled into the water. Wide fissures opened in the earth; when they closed, a darkish liquid sprayed into the air, higher than the trees. Geysers spouted, hurling up shale, sand, and water. Foul-smelling sulphur gases and lumps of coal spewed up from beneath the riverbed. The Mississippi rose and swirled and became lumpy with snags and rotted trees lifted from its bottom. At one point it reversed its course and flowed backward, filling a large area of northwestern Tennessee which was lower than the river. This action formed an eighteen-mile-long lake in the depressed area, leaving many trees along the river bent in an upstream direction. In short, New Madrid was the approximate center for what is generally considered America's most severe nonvolcanic earth shock.

The initial tremors brought terror to the residents of New Madrid, many of whom believed the event signaled the end of the world and that every portion of the nation was experiencing the same turmoil. A New Madrid schoolmistress, awakened when her bed was slammed into a wall, later wrote that "in one person, a female, the alarm was so great that she fainted and could not be revived." Some men hurriedly cut down large trees and placed them at right angles to the direction of fissures cutting across the earth. They sat on the trees, hoping that the trunks would span any chasms, thus keeping them from falling into the seemingly bottomless cracks. Organizing a torchlight march, some residents rushed to a hill seven miles west of the river. There they built a huge bonfire and in English, French, and Spanish prayed to God for deliverance. With the ground rocking and the smell of sulphur rising, they feared that at any moment fire would leap from the earth to consume everything.

Tremors of varying power continued until mid-March. A man in Louisville counted a total of 1,874 shocks, eight of which he scaled among the most severe of six classes of intensity. Houses, men, boats, and animals were swept away by the water; some disappeared into the fissures. Surveying the ravaged communities and torn earth, one traveler commented that "all nature appeared in ruins, and seemed to mourn in a solitude over her melancholy fate." By spring the earth shock was finally exhausted, and it was business as usual along the river—so much so, in fact, that one man chided the residents of New Madrid for "not even checking their dancing, frolics, and vices."

Ironically, the year 1811 also marked a major turning point in the development of the Mississippi. In the fall of that year, Nicholas I. Roosevelt, a partner of Robert Fulton and Robert Livingston, set out from Pittsburgh in a side-wheeler constructed at a cost of $38,000. His goal was New Orleans and a steamboat monopoly on the Mississippi for the Fulton-Livingston combine.

A brother of President Theodore Roosevelt's grandfather, Roosevelt had the shrewdness and determination so characteristic of the family. Skeptics said the ungainly vessel with the large sidewheels would never survive the Falls of the Ohio rocks, and if it accomplished that, it could never generate enough power to run upstream against currents of the Ohio or the Mississippi. Added to these difficulties, Roosevelt was taking his pregnant wife on the voyage. He was denounced as "foolhardy" for initiating the trip and harangued for his "inconsiderate care" of Mrs. Roosevelt. The vessel, named the *New Orleans,* pushed on, carrying the Roosevelts, a captain, a pilot, an engineer, six hands, a waiter, a cook, two servants for Mrs. Roosevelt, and Tiger, the family's giant Newfoundland dog.

Crowds turned out along the Ohio to see the vessel. The mayor of Cincinnati told Roosevelt: "You have visited us in a steamboat, but we see you for the last time. Your boat may go down the river, but as to coming up, the very idea is an absurd one." Roosevelt heard the same words in Louisville, and set out to prove the doubters wrong. Community leaders were invited to visit the *New Orleans,* and as they sat down to a banquet, the vessel began to tremble and move in the water. The guests rushed topside, and to their dismay found the *New Orleans* moving effortlessly upstream, against the current. While waiting for higher water at the treacherous Falls of Ohio, Roosevelt ran back upstream to Cincinnati to show the disbelievers that the impossible was possible.

Late in November, Roosevelt decided to brave the falls. Accompanied by two pilots experienced with the rapids, the *New Orleans* set off for its major test. The key to success was generating a speed faster than the current. Hitting the rapids, the vessel spun, dipped, and rolled, but the speed was maintained, and the rapids cleared. It looked like clear steaming to Natchez and New Orleans.

But the run over the rapids was immediately followed by the New Madrid earthquake. The vessel shuddered against ocean-sized waves, barely eluding huge trees slicing through the water, avoiding islands created overnight, and groping through new and uncharted channels.

Along the river, terrified settlers shouted for the *New Orleans* to turn back. Others begged permission to come aboard to escape the collapsing earth. Seeing the smoke-spouting vessel as a bad omen, Indians called it *Penelore,* or "fire canoe." Early in January the vessel reached Natchez, where the cheering population turned out to greet the historic arrival. One Negro is said to have tossed his hat in the air and exclaimed, "Ole Mississippi done got her marster now!"

The age of steam had reached the Mississippi.

It was a glorious age. It has been estimated that four thousand steamboats—with an average lifespan of five years—plied the Mississippi before the end of the century. The vessels that followed the *New Orleans* evolved into massive creatures of power and luxury. Perhaps the finest was the *J. M. White,* which was graced with stained glass, statuary, gilt chandeliers, and an octagonal-domed barroom. The historian Walter Havighurst has noted that "from her heart of oak keel to her 2,880-pound roof bell, her five-tone whistle, and the seven-foot ornamental leaves on her eight-foot chimneys, she was the queen of the river. All her china showed her own handsome picture. Her Irish linen was monogramed J M W, and her silver was engraved with her twin-stacked silhouette."

But the river traffic, mounting after the Civil War, began to shift from the steamboat to the railroads. Protected by the levees, the railroads thrived and pushed into the Deep South. Mark Twain noted in 1882 that "there is a locomotive in sight from the deck of the steamboat almost the whole way from St. Louis to St. Paul." By 1876 virtually all passenger traffic between St. Louis and the South was by rail. Looking back at the period, William Faulkner wrote: "There were railroads in the wilderness now. People who used to go over land by carriage or on horseback to the river landings for the Memphis and New Orleans steamboats could take the train from almost anywhere." Freight also shifted to the railroads. In 1886 Memphis was shipping four times as much cotton by rail as by river. In December of that year, while tied up at a plantation in Louisiana, the *J. M. White* burned. Only twisted steel was left of her nobility. The brief but glorious age of steamboating on the Mississippi was coming to an end.

Route 61 follows the Mississippi on the west bank, passing through a series of nondescript towns until it reaches Wilson, which sits like an immaculate English village in the dull and flat Arkansas cotton country. The vivid green town square is surrounded by neat red-brick buildings, braced by thick timbers and graced by cupolas and wide windows. Wilson is headquarters of Lee Wilson and Company, operators of the largest family-owned cotton plantation in the South. The 33,000-acre plantation began in 1886 when Robert Edward Lee Wilson rented some swampy land off the river and began to cut timber. Unlike timber operators who like to cut and run, Wilson thought the "plow should follow the saw." He drained his cleared land and went into farming. Steadily acquiring property, Wilson, his son, and grandson developed an agricultural empire augmented by a variety of modern enterprises, ranging from an auto dealership to a seed export firm and to service stations in the three towns on the plantation.

It used to be said that "Mr. Wilson owns everything in town but the railroad station, and his name's on that." But the firm is now selling homes and branching out into such new endeavors as a thirty-thousand-acre cattle ranch in Nevada. Robert Edward Lee Wilson III heads a company that changes with the nature of the industry. A photograph in company headquarters shows a cotton-laden train steaming off from Wilson to market after the 1919 harvest. The cars are piled high with fluffy white cotton, with men sitting atop each car to beat out sparks that flew back from the steam engine. It was a one-million-dollar load.

Wilson, Arkansas [and facing page]

"That same amount of cotton would today be worth about half of what it was at that time," said Hudson Wren, vice-president and general manager of the operation.

"Synthetics do that to the cotton price?"

"My, that's an ugly word," chuckled Wren. "Don't say that word around here."

While the Wilson plantation in a recent year had 11,800 acres in cotton, it also had 15,500 acres in soybeans. Other products range from rice and wheat to collards and turnip greens. In the island of technology that the plantation has become, it was reassuring to see a battered old bi-wing airplane, looking only slightly more modern than a mule, charging over the fields, dispelling a misty cloud of chemical fertilizer onto the turf. Painted a defiant shade of orange, the plane would suddenly unleash a roar of power, lift over the road and telephone wires, then once again settle down to ground level. The furrows it serviced were straight, as though laid out by a T-square. The only sense of terrain came from the wires and meager shacks spotted without pattern across the fields. Most of the buildings were deserted, but outside one, an old Negro man was slowly chopping at a pile of logs. Except for the thud of the ax and the rustle of wind through weeds along the asphalt, all was still. A low hum announced the plane's return. The hum escalated into a roar as the plane streaked across the field, rose over the wires, completed the next field, then banked above a levee for a return run. After another series of passes, it glided into a field where a tank truck refueled it. Apart from a faded old wind sock sagging from a pole near a makeshift hangar, the landing field was a clear stretch of unencumbered land.

The pilot, Charles Tuminello, climbed easily from his open cockpit, jumped off the wing, and started walking toward the hangar. He wore a World War I–style cloth flight cap, a drab jump suit, and gloves. "Those things aren't easy to fly," he said, "but they're dependable." Tuminello has been crop dusting for a dozen years. "This old plane takes a lot of punishment. We spray about ten months of the year. Some planting. Some fertilizing. Sometimes you fly at two or three feet. Sometimes at thirty. You got to watch out for high wind and high humidity. Then there's that dead air. No lift to it. That's when you can catch the trouble. But I don't think it's as dangerous as some people make it out to be. You can get on a pair of roller skates and break your neck. So I don't worry about it."

Tuminello got into his plane and took off. The young black operating the truck knew Tuminello would be back for another load of fertilizer in six to eight minutes, so he stretched out in the shade.

"Ever think of flying one of those?"

"They ain't for me. No, sir! I'm heading on up to Chicago soon to drive a truck. You'll never catch this boy in one of those dusters."

It was a quiet, warm Memorial Day afternoon in Memphis, Tennessee. Flags hung limply along vacant streets where the silence was broken only by the hoarse cough of a bus trailing a cloud of exhaust fumes. Memphis is set on high, flood-free bluffs overlooking the Mississippi and its waterfront. While downtown Memphis shows little relationship to the river, the waterfront below the bluffs hints strongly at the romance of the Mississippi. The waterfront, formed of stones set into the earth, slants steeply down to the river. The stones have been worn smooth, partly by mosquito-tormented mules pulling wagons of cotton bales, partly by pale and emaciated soldiers on the way home from the Civil War, partly by elegant travelers stepping from steamboat "cabin carpets as soft as mush" into the turbulence of a town that for years experienced the rowdy influence of the rivermen. Sam Jones, an evangelist involved in one of the many futile attempts to clean up the city, once declared that "if whiskey ran ankle deep in Memphis and each front door had a dipper tied to it, you could not get drunker quicker than you can in Memphis now." Another startled traveler observed that "the only difference between Memphis and hell is that Memphis has a river running alongside it."

Memphis has experienced its hells—a Civil War that left it exhausted and demoralized, three yellow fever epidemics within a decade, a long period of economic and political atrophy. But contemporary Memphis has emerged as a major commercial center in the mid-South, and there is little evidence here of the languor long associated with the South. But on Memorial Day, with the temperature climbing into the nineties, Memphis was under a siege of drowsiness.

Memphis [and following pages]

People who visited the Memphis National Cemetery for Memorial Day Services clustered under the tall, imperial trees. For the most part they tended to be old, proud, and polite. The men dressed conservatively, with precisely folded handkerchiefs in vest pockets and immaculate white shirts. Some wore black-and-white shoes. The women tended toward the pale and frumpy, with fluffy white hair and patterned, light-colored dresses. By the exuberance of the greetings exchanged, it seemed most of these people met only once a year, at the Memorial Day services—and possibly another time or two when they were united at the funeral of a friend.

As they waited for the service to begin, a few people left the comfort of the shade to wander down the long parallel rows of headstones. After a few minutes, however, they were driven by the unrelenting sun back to the comfort of the trees. The tombstones in the Memphis National Cemetery provide a stark history of the last century of American military engagements. Founded in 1867, the cemetery immediately received the remains of 8,866 unidentified men who died in the effort to preserve the Union. Freshly turned earth and recently wilted flowers represented the graves of three young Americans who died in Vietnam and were buried shortly before Memorial Day.

The cemetery also marks the final resting place for many victims of the *Sultana* tragedy. The once resplendent steamboat *Sultana*, depleted by two years of unrelieved labor during the Civil War, set out from Memphis on the night of April 26, 1865. Originally designed to carry seventy-six cabin passengers and three hundred deck passengers and crewmen, on this night the *Sultana* held 2,400 Union soldiers recently released from the Confederate stockades at Andersonville and Cahaba.

Memorial Day, Memphis [and following pages]

The soldiers, battered, emanciated, ill, and many of them maimed, were jubilant in spite of the crowded conditions. They were en route to Cairo, and from there, by trains and wagons and on foot, to the farms and villages of Indiana, Illinois, Ohio, and Michigan. For them it was the end of the war. About seven miles north of Memphis, in a stretch of the Mississippi expanded to nine miles in width by flooding, a massive explosion convulsed the *Sultana*. As all three decks of the vessel were ripped open, bodies flew into the air. Other men were killed by scalding steam, collapsing smokestacks, and ricocheting planks. Rather than die in the fire, still others leaped to certain death in the swirling water. Through luck or imagination, some survived. Three men who were blown from the vessel landed on a slab of wood from the hurricane deck and floated downstream to Memphis. One soldier remembered Sully, a ten-foot pet alligator kept by the *Sultana* crew as a mascot. "When the blowup came," he said afterward, "I crawled down to the deck below and just happened to remember where that alligator was hidden . . . you see, the crew of the *Sultana* kept this vicious-looking critter in a stout wooden cage. I jerked open the door and ran my bayonet through him three times. Then I dumped him out of his box and dragged it out on the deck and pushed it over. Made a mighty fine boat. Just fit me. I floated till I hung up on some willow trees in shallow water." Such survival stories, however, were tragically rare. Within twenty minutes the *Sultana* was a fiery coffin and approximately 1,500 men went under with her. With the change in the river channel over the years, as late as 1954 farmers plowed a cotton field around her protruding jack staff.

After the young girls in Brownie uniforms passed out programs, the memorial service got underway with a pledge to the flag. The two hundred participants sat on folding chairs, nestled in the shade around a speaker's platform decked out in red, white, and blue bunting. The speaker, a former Congressman, gave an impassioned address, denouncing war protesters, campus protesters, and disrespect for the flag. After the speeches and prayers, a flag was placed at the grave of an unknown soldier. The sound of taps flowed across this vast field of sorrow.

A tall, well-dressed black woman, with two small children clutching at her skirt, began to sob. The children looked down at the earth. The trio seemed helpless, and alone. Two white women walked over to console the woman, who slowly regained her composure.

Beale Street is a narrow street that runs perpendicular to the Mississippi on the south side of Memphis' downtown district. It is a gaudy commercial street in a black slum. In its pawnshop windows shiny watches and glistening guitars are displayed behind sliding steel grates. Merchants sit outside their stores on shiny black footlockers, attempting to entice pedestrians inside. Jaunty young blacks walk by in garish-colored slacks and cocky berets. There is talk of urban renewal which will restore Beale Street as an entertainment center, a shrine to the birth of the blues, and to W. C. Handy, the "Father of the Blues."

Born in 1873 on Handy's Hill in Florence, Alabama, the son and grandson of Methodist ministers, Handy began making music by "scraping a twenty-penny nail across the teeth of the jawbone of a horse that had died in the woods nearby." In school he learned the classics—Wagner, Bizet, Verdi—but a greater impression was made by the music of his race. At thirteen he purchased an old cornet for $1.75. His father despaired, saying, "You are trotting down to hell on a fast horse in a porcupine saddle." Handy stayed with music, and in 1903 became music director of the Negro Knights of Pythias band in Clarksdale, Mississippi. Clarksdale was then the heart of the blues country in the Mississippi Delta. The blacks of the cotton country were singing of their dreams and disappointments, of love, mules, work in the fields, steamboats, hard liquor and skimpy food, of birth and death, and women—good women, fickle women, fast women.

Eventually all the songs and singers got to Clarksdale. "They sauntered into town by way of the railroad tracks," Handy recalled, "or were dropped from freight cars or caught rides on the big road and entered town on the tops of cotton bales. Once in Clarksdale, they played and sang anywhere they could find an audience: on street corners or along the busiest sidewalks. A favorite hangout was the railroad station, where they could pour out their hearts in song while the audience ate fish and bread, chewed sugar cane, and dipped snuff while waiting for trains to carry them down the line."

Handy took those songs, with their emotions and universal truths, and put them into a form that appealed to the popular tastes of the day. Commercially, Handy took the blues from the cotton fields and the Clarksdale railroad depot and refined them into a form that Tin Pan Alley could merchandise. In Memphis, Handy initially worked out of Pee Wee's Cafe at 317 Beale at a time when the street lived twenty-four hours a day with gamblers, entertainers, dandies, big spenders, and beautiful women. The music is today gone from Beale Street, which was closed down during a World War II reform movement and has never reopened.

Robert Henry is seventy-nine and one of the few old-timers left on the street. He runs a pool hall where you can sip a soft drink and get your shoes shined while watching the players go to it on the string of tables in his long, narrow shop. Henry is a slight, light-complexioned (his father was white, his mother black) man, who sits on a bench along the wall watching the activity. His patrons seem good natured; bragging and challenges and epithets are vigorous but friendly. But there is no trace of the silk toppers and Prince Alberts once common on Beale Street. This is the working class.

"This street has been a good street," Henry declared. "A good, good, good street. Now, it's a forgotten street. The church people here won't let you do nothing any more. They're against everything. It used to be wide open in this town. At 1 A.M. the street was packed. The better class of people used to come to Beale Street. There's no music here, now. Just records. And people are afraid to come down here. These young kids wear yellow, green, and blue pants. You know. The ones with those little whiskers and chains around their necks. Bad ones.

"I met Handy hanging around on the street. I used to do a lot of drawing and put some sketches on his music stands. He was the most human guy you could meet. He was loved by the white people of this city, too. He was a humdinger."

Henry paused as a young black police officer walked into the shop. The policeman stopped at the front door and scanned the dim room until he saw Henry, then walked toward him. Henry grew nervous. The officer pulled out a pad and scrawled out the name of a dog. He ripped off the piece of paper and handed it to Henry along with two one-dollar bills.

"How are you today, Mr. Henry?" the officer inquired.

"Mighty fine. And you?"

"Good." The officer walked out, and Henry stuffed the paper and bills in his pocket.

"Do you make book in here, Mr. Henry?"

"Never," he answered, appearing hurt that anyone would suggest such a thing. "I'll just place a bet for that good man at the dog track tonight. That's all. You better not do nothing in this town."

Walking back toward the downtown, one passes the statue of Handy in a skimpy little park. Pee Wee's Cafe at 317 Beale Street is now a pool hall graced by a large "Enjoy Double Cola" sign. On one side is a sleazy club, on the other an abandoned photo store. A burned-out building is nearby. Across town a new generation of prosperous musicians is turning out soul music for Stax-Volt records. But Beale Street is dead, and the do-gooders have won a total victory over a legend.

South of Memphis, it becomes obvious that when it came to topography, Arkansas was shortchanged. On the east bank of the Mississippi are bluffs which allowed for the development of such towns as Memphis, Vicksburg, and Natchez, but on the west bank, the Arkansas side, it is generally low and swampy. Those who crossed to the west bank either had to push inland or stay close to the river and face the threats of low land and high water. Those threats were braved at Napoleon, a town situated at the point where the Mississippi receives the Arkansas River. It was once a promising town, a county seat, with a large government hospital. But the two rivers gnawed away at Napoleon. When a building owner got nervous about the river, he abandoned his building and rebuilt on the far side of town. But the Mississippi would not be denied, and the residents of Napoleon finally surrendered their town to the river. Today there is no trace of the town.

Helena, Arkansas, sits securely behind a levee, with its few gracious homes on high land. On a warm Sunday morning a group of young men were standing outside a brick church in the black section of town. Elijah Mondy, a Helena native who had lived in Chicago (known locally as "the promised land") was attempting to persuade his friends that Helena was a more desirable place than Chicago.

Near Helena, Arkansas

Helena [and following pages]

"It's nicer here," Mondy insisted. "The people here aren't crude. They are more relaxed and warm. Nobody here is going to slip up behind you and zip you in the back with a knife. If a boy is hungry here, somebody will feed him."

"I don't dig it, Elijah," one young man answered. "The cops here are harassing us college kids when we're home. They think we're going to start a revolution or something. It's depressing. Half the kids here won't ever see anything in their lives but Helena. You've got kids here in three-room houses that are the same houses the same family has lived in for three generations."

"So these kids should go to Chicago and get in classrooms with sixty other kids? What are they going to learn there? You don't read me. The people here in Helena are a lot more human. In Chicago it takes a calamity, like a big snow, to bring that out."

A tall, muscular youth stood at the edge of the crowd. On one wrist he wore a slender gold bracelet of the type the mountain tribesmen of South Vietnam give to Americans they respect.

"Look around here, Elijah," he said. "At least one or two kids have drowned here this year in the big ditch [the Mississippi]. But the sign outside the swimming pool over there says "Private." You know what that means: Keep out, nigger. The Negroes here are economically owned by the whites. So they won't speak out. If they do, no jobs, no bread. We aren't getting any leadership from our parents. The movement is passing us by."

The discussion went on until the older people came out of the church and started walking home, down the dusty streets in front of small, colorless houses mounted on cement blocks. The older people don't like to hear the young people talking about such matters. So the young people look away, past the drab houses, past the houses on the hill, to the promised land that Elijah claims is short on delivery.

Farther south is Arkansas City, which stands forlornly behind a levee. Arkansas City is a prime illustration of the barn door being locked after the horse was stolen. "The flood came here in 1927," said the man in a tiny municipal museum. "I had eight to ten feet of water in my house. That was the death blow for Arkansas City." After the completion of a secure levee, townspeople talked enthusiastically of industrial development and tourism. But Arkansas City has languished; today it is a meager town of weed-filled lots, abandoned buildings, and little stores.

Arkansas City, Arkansas

"The '27 water sure messed up this town," said an old black sitting in the shade of a store porch. "I'm fifty years old and work myself to death these days. I got a houseful of children . . . ten of my own and one grandkid. I try to have the old TV going and I got my radio fixed. I get $1.25 an hour when I work, but when it rains and I can't work, then I go into debt to the man and you know what that means. I can't get a public job. They don't take a man my age with one eye. I got into a little fret one night and got cut. I beat the man who did it with a club after he cut me. I tore his ass up but it hasn't brought back my eye."

Traveling south, car tires slap rhythmically against the black lines of soggy tar on aging concrete. The trees seem heavy in foliage; the grass grows thick and so rapidly, men inevitably fall behind in all attempts to control it. Sometimes they just ignore it. Shacks sit several hundred feet off the road, at the edge of cotton fields which drop back to trees and underbrush that signal the levee and, beyond, the Mississippi. The field out back is carefully tended; in the field next to the highway, the grass grows with a voraciousness that consumes discarded shoes and toys and even the hulk of a long-expired pickup truck. Screens over the door and the two front windows of a shack hang precariously. A family sits on the front porch, which sags toward the middle as though it would spring back to level if the family stepped into the yard. The people stare at the passing cars. In anger? Envy? Boredom? How does a black family consigned to a shack on the edge of the industrial revolution react, or even relate, to a white family in an air-conditioned car speeding toward the next frisson of tourism?

Where a spread of hot white gravel and two gasoline pumps mark a roadside stop, bright tin signs lent life to a shabby wooden store building cringing in the sun. A lanky, tired-looking man lounged in the shade of the front porch, his back resting against a flimsy pillar. A soft-drink bottle propped against his chest formed a moist circle of sweat on the cloth.

"Head'n' ta New Orleans?" he asked, taking a swig.

"Ya. But in no hurry."

"Better find some. It'll be a hot 'un today. That highway'll heat up on ya."

Vicksburg, Mississippi [and following page]

"You traveling, too?"

"No. Goin' home. Been out all night. No luck."

"Fishing?"

"Not that way. I'm a warden." He had spent the night on the Mississippi, attempting to catch a band of fishermen who use an electrical device that stuns the fish to the surface for easy harvesting.

"They can fill up a boat in short order with that old trick. Drop in a wire, turn the crank and that's it. The ones they don't get don't ever reproduce again. But we're gettin' to 'em, breakin' 'em up. Mighty fast. I've been on this job now for nine, ten years. There's improvement along this river. Even with more fishin' and huntin' both. The violations—the ones that hurt us bad—aren't so many these days. People are begin' to understand this conservation business. They used to resent it more."

Vicksburg is a prosperous little town that was separated from the Mississippi in 1876 when the river broke across a curve and left the town about three miles from the channel. Army engineers diverted the lower part of the Yazoo River, which emptied into the river above Vicksburg, into the old Mississippi channel so the town would have access to the big river. It would be impossible, however, to isolate Vicksburg from its historical relationship to the Mississippi.

During the bustling days of King Cotton, Vicksburg was a thriving community which attracted more than its share of the river's riffraff. The local citizenry was occasionally obliged to purge the ne'er-do-wells. When a successful young planter failed to survive a trip to a gambling den in 1835, the do-gooders declared that anyone unable to display an ability to earn an honest living had twenty-four hours to clear out of town. There was a quite explicit message for gamblers: "Such persons found within the town limits after the expiration of this time shall receive thirty-nine lashes at the public whipping post." Most gamblers got the word, but five of them decided to ride out this burst of civic indignation. They were unceremoniously hanged and buried at the foot of the town gallows.

Illinois Central, Mississippi

Vicksburg [and following pages]

Vicksburg still has a few imposing homes from antebellum days, and the town's old courthouse contains an extensive collection of Americana from that period. Moored at the waterfront is the stern-wheeler *Sprague,* the world's largest towboat. Now utilized as a showboat by a local theater group, in 1907 the *Sprague* set an all-time record for towing—a sixty-unit tow that covered six and one-half acres and carried 67,307 tons of coal. Rivermen estimate it would take 1,500 railroad cars to handle that load.

Up from the waterfront, on Washington Street, there is an old garage building with a "Closed" sign in the window. But if you rap insistently on the glass, Brooks Farrish will walk haltingly to the door and let you in. He is eighty-two, and since his brother Frank, eighty, fell into bad health, the little curio and junk shop has been semi-closed.

As he talked, Brooks used a penknife to scrape tough pieces of flesh from a raccoon hide. "The niggers catch them down in the swamp," he explained, throwing the pelt onto a pile of brown and gray fur heaped in a corner. "We buy the hides and someone else down the way buys the meat. We pay about a dollar for the hide. Some we sell for one and a half, others for seventy-five cents. We come out a bit ahead. Not much else to do now." To the rear of the shop is an old sedan, covered by a smooth, thick layer of gray dust. There are also books ("We couldn't sell *Lady Chatterly* in this town") and guns ("We haven't got a good Civil War gun from the battlefield for seven or eight years") and bottles (what appears to be an ornate beer bottle is offered at $1.50). In a cigar box behind the counter Brooks has some slugs and rifle balls taken from the earth at the Vicksburg National Military Park.

"They're putting through a road up here and some boys on the bulldozers saw these and brought them in here. Those hills are something."

It was on those hills that one of the most savage, and certainly one of the most decisive, battles of the Civil War was fought. Early in the struggle the Confederacy, underestimating the immense strategic and economic value of the Mississippi, left it relatively unprotected. The Union, seeing the conquest of the Mississippi as a means of splitting the South while opening the river for military and commercial traffic, set forth to banish the Confederates from the waterway. By the summer of 1862, New Orleans and Memphis were under the Stars and Stripes. But Vicksburg, from its commanding bluffs overlooking a loop in the river, remained a Confederate bastion. Its smoothbore cannon and rifled guns could devastate river traffic. General U. S. Grant, leading the Union Army of the Tennessee, originally approached Vicksburg from the north, but was repulsed. Grant then maneuvered down the west bank of the river, crossed back into Mississippi south of Vicksburg, and struck out toward the northeast. After a series of engagements, his troops sacked Jackson, a vital communications center, and then moved west toward Vicksburg, routing its Confederate defenders.

On May 18 the Southern troops under Lieutenant General J. C. Pemberton were forced back within the defenses at the rear of Vicksburg. The defenses were built into ridges that formed a crescent around the town. A great siege was underway. With Union vessels firing at Vicksburg from the river, and Grant's troops assaulting from the west, the early collapse of Vicksburg seemed inevitable. But after heavy fighting the Union charges were turned back. Grant then decided to starve out the defenders. By the end of June the Confederate soldiers' diet was down to a stale biscuit and one piece of fat bacon a day. Mule meat was a delicacy. An officer told Pemberton: "This army is ripe for mutiny unless it can be fed." On July 4, Pemberton surrendered his 31,000 troops. With the surrender of Vicksburg, the Mississippi was open, cotton could be shipped north to the mills, and the South was torn asunder. Both spiritually and geographically, the loss of Vicksburg was the death blow to the Confederacy.

Kitty Kat Club, Vicksburg [and following pages]

Most of the battlefield is now within the 1,323-acre Vicksburg National Military Park. Many of the original fortifications and trenches are intact; others have been duplicated to re-create the topography during the height of the carnage. The fields are dotted with historical markers which chart the positions of engaged units and the path of attacks. One can start from a Union encampment and, following the markers, trace the progression of the trenches that took boys from Iowa and Ohio close enough to a Confederate redan, or triangular fort, to exchange hand grenades with boys from Alabama and Texas. On a sunny winter afternoon, as one strolls across the hills along a chain of markers, it is easy to imagine the frantic, chaotic charges amid the piercing shrieks of the wounded and dying, and the cacophony of cannons and rifles. It is said that at night boys fighting on opposite sides, from the same town in Missouri, would meet to discuss the latest news from home and then quietly wish one another good luck in the next day's fighting. A tribute to that engagement declares: "Here brothers fought for their principles. Here heroes died for their country. And a united people will forever cherish the precious legacy of their noble manhood."

At Fort Gibson you turn right and travel for several miles along a winding road that becomes, in effect, a tunnel through thick stands of trees drooping with moss. At the end is an eerie view of columns, at least two stories tall, marking off the outline of a majestic home that at one time overlooked the Mississippi. Cows now graze across what was once an elegant lawn. Next to one line of columns is a shack. A woman and her children walk out of the shack and start off toward a nearby stream. The children are laughing; the woman seems relaxed and happy.

A plaque tells the familiar story: Windsor, a showplace home built by six hundred slaves; imported furniture, carpets, marble, glass; bountiful cotton acreage; shrill salutes from steamboats pulling into the plantation landing; a gala party followed by a night of fire which left the stark columns for history. Ambitious vegetation climbs some of the columns; a tree grows nonchalantly from the top of another; others are bare, chunks of concrete having fallen out, exposing a core of brick. A few are joined at the top by a strand of twisted ironwork.

Vicksburg [and following pages]

We walked cautiously through the square, examining little chunks of stone and marble. A black man appeared at the door of the shack, turning his head to the right and pressing his ear up against the screen. He pulled back from the door and called out, "My eyes have failed me, and my family's out back."

Soon he again moved to the door, his good ear again pushed close to the screen.

"I'm not able to do nothing now," he said. "I'm at the mercy of everybody."

"Have you lived here long?"

"I was born on this place in 1902. The family that owns it is all but died out. An heir in town owns the place now. He's going to let it stand like it is. He sold off all the land, but he won't sell this. It's not bad here. I've only known one of the columns to fall in my time. My grandfather was a slave on this plantation. They had six hundred slaves here. But I don't know where the slave quarter was . . . or even where they all were buried. Couple of years ago, with my eyes good, I could find Granddaddy's grave. It was way down near the river, but that's all changed now, they say. Even with eyes I don't think I could find it now.

"You know they made a movie here. *Raintree County* it was called. I helped fix the place up for that. Now that was really something. It doesn't look like much now, I guess. But people come by every day. This is my home. I feel I should be home."

Windsor plantation today clings to a pitiful life, occupied by a blind black whose unwilling ancestors brought it to birth with their labor. But the mansions in the town of Natchez have survived war and fire and commercial decline, and provide the underpinning for the town's slogan: "Where the Old South Still Lives." To be at home today in Windsor is at best ironical; to be at home in one of the mansions of Natchez is to be alive in a dream that survived the reality of more than one hundred years of history. Natchez is unique in America. It is a town where the past and present have become hopelessly confused, where the past is celebrated in the present, and where the present is dedicated to resurrecting the past. The thousands of visitors who annually traipse through the old homes must, for a few fleeting moments at least, picture themselves as dashing planters or enchanting belles in an aristocratic world devoid of cares. Natchez is dedicated to fostering that fantasy. Fantasy, indeed, is its very lifeblood.

Natchez [and following pages]

"Natchez is a place for the intelligent," said Mrs. J. Balfour Miller, who has played a key role in the development of Natchez. "It's a place for people who adore art, antiques, furniture, china . . . it is a place for people who are receptive to beauty. As one visitor told me, 'It's a dream.' We set the stage for a dream."

Mrs. Miller is at once gracious, polite; complimentary, aloof, demure —and hard as nails. Frail and seventy-five, she is nevertheless inexhaustible when charging through a Natchez showplace. She drives her large Buick through the town's narrow streets with a courage that would have befitted a colonel of the Confederate cavalry. More than a quarter of a century ago she began booming Natchez, giving lectures about its unique homes. "In the beginning, even the Mississippi people didn't know what we had here. We were an unknown quantity. I'd give lectures and go see the newspaper people. I was very good at vamping the newspaper people." Mrs. Miller gave the lectures, generated the publicity, encouraged the rehabilitation of the houses, and generally developed the past as a commercial resource.

As it happens, Natchez' past is dramatic. The French initially built a fort at the site, taking advantage of the two-hundred-foot bluffs above the Mississippi. The land then passed from the French to the English to the Spanish and finally to the Americans. The cotton plantations brought wealth—at one time Natchez was reportedly second only to New York in its number of resident millionaires—and elegant living. One extravagant planter provided hand-carved mahogany stalls for his racehorses. They drank from marble troughs, and a large mirror was installed in each stall so the resident beast could admire his own countenance.

While those on the hill lived the good life, the scum of the lower Mississippi gathered below at the river's edge in a community of scoundrels and cutthroats known as Natchez-Under-the-Hill. Many a traveler heading north lost his purse there, and ended up walking toward home over the Natchez Trace (old French for "a line of footprints"), a tree-stump-dotted path running from Natchez to Nashville, where it connected with routes north.

Captain John Russell once docked his steamboat, the *Constellation,* in front of an Under-the-Hill dive. The travelers strolled out to view the bizarre life, and one of them, a minister, explaining he was gathering material for sermons, took a fling at the gaming table. The resident sinners showed little tolerance for the cloth, and the man of God was wiped out. He promptly complained to Captain Russell, who stormed ashore and demanded of the gambling house proprietor that the minister's funds be returned.

"Now, I just cain't do that," the proprietor lamented. "After all, it was a game of chance, and he took a chance like anybody else."

"He took a chance with thieves," the captain declared. "You didn't win his money. You stole it. You return that money or I'll dump your whole outfit in the river."

"High and mighty, ain't you? That would be right interestin'. I'd like to see you try it."

The captain dispatched a group of army deckhands to shore. They passed a chain around the building and attached it to the capstan of the *Constellation.* The gamblers laughed until Captain Russell rang the *Constellation* full speed astern, pulling the house down the bank into the water. "Stop!" the owner shrieked. "I'll pay." The minister got his money back, and went into folklore as one of the few innocents to visit Natchez-Under-the-Hill and survive.

There are thirty homes on the annual Natchez pilgrimage, which was initiated by Mrs. Miller, and it takes three days to complete the tour. Mrs. Miller lives in one of the homes, Hope Farm, which sits on a hill in the midst of a garden shaded by pecan trees and enormous oaks. A portion of the house was built in 1789 by a Spanish governor. Most of the homes have romantic histories, and a surprising number have been in the same families for generations.

Mrs. Miller is particularly annoyed by stories of Southerners' mistreating slaves. "This is where they whipped the slaves," she commented caustically during a tour of Hope Hill. "One visitor asked if our grandparents whipped slaves. I nearly died. First of all, nobody whipped slaves. If they did, they were ostracized."

Mrs. Miller is also bewildered by what she considers the "negative" attitudes of some young blacks. "We are really one family with our colored," she said. "But the young colored people don't know about the past. We were left with the Negroes on our hands after the Civil War. We didn't have any money. My grandmother would give the old slaves whatever she had, and she didn't have much. The young don't understand that part. They all have TV and hear about those terrible things in the North."

It hardly needs to be said that Natchez' blacks don't share Mrs. Miller's zeal about the pilgrimage and the annual pageant which includes "pictures from our treasured past." The story depicts joyful white children frolicking about the large-columned galleries of Dunleith plantation, Jefferson Davis marrying Varina Howell at the Briars, the sound of slaves down in the fields singing spirituals, and gallant soldiers dashing off to war to the sound of "Dixie." One black said of the celebrants: "They got themselves so confused that when they lookin' at the pageant they think they watchin' a newsreel, and that we still in the fields pickin' cotton."

South of Natchez, the Mississippi flexes its muscles and expands
to shove against the banks and into the vulnerable countryside. The
levees here give the river a wide berth, and communities and roads
keep a prudent distance from the main channel. As one moves down
the river, between miles and miles of forests and swamps, there is
little evidence of human presence along the shore. The river
achieves a sense of privacy, which is quickly lost at Baton Rouge,
the capital of Louisiana, where people and industry once again take
a toehold on the waterway. Tugboats, ocean freighters, and tankers
become commonplace; Baton Rouge thrives on oil, and has large
refineries and chemical plants. As the Mississippi churns on toward
New Orleans, the commercial activity increases. North of Baton
Rouge there is a transition from flat black earth to rich, red rolling
hills. These red hills are the calling card for southern Louisiana, one
of the most delightfully bizarre portions of America. *American
Heritage,* the magazine, once prepared a recipe for its cultural
makeup:

> "Take a cup of Choctaw and add Frenchmen, Adventuriers de
> Bois and Acadian refugees from Nova Scotia
>
> "Blend in a Mississippi Bubble, a sprinkling of fugitives from
> justice, and a few Filles de Joie
>
> "Now sift in Catalans, Spanish planters, Gens de Couleur, and
> a Gombo Negre
>
> "Make a Code Noir and some Quadroon Balls
>
> "Stir together gently, adding Dalmatian oystermen, Filipino
> shrimpers, Germans, and 'Kaintucks' (often rather tough)
>
> "Add a pinch of pirates
>
> "Simmer slowly under six flags
>
> "Serves most of southern Louisiana."

The excitement of this mixture is lost along the standard entrance
to New Orleans. One passes down a neon highway, an explosion
of plastic franchises, which initially reduces New Orleans to the
aesthetic status of a main drag in suburban Indianapolis. But once
in the city, this sense of sameness disappears. People are strikingly
polite, offering a casual and quick friendliness sorely lacking in so
many other cities. The Vieux Carré, literally the "old square,"
provides pleasurable hours for the serendipitist.

New Orleans [and following pages]

At night, New Orleans thrives with an intensity that tourists find irresistible. You can sit on a hard chair in a humid, oppressively hot hall listening to frail old black musicians play traditional New Orleans jazz, and then walk around the corner to a bar where a bored tout straddles the sidewalk proclaiming the intoxicating charms of "Baby Doll, all 337 pounds of her, the biggest stripper in the world." Baby Doll turns out to be an elephantine woman done up in a sequined G-string and tassels who pants and sweats as she struggles through bumps and grinds under lights that turn her pale flesh a variety of ghastly colors. The men in the booths shout vulgarities, while their wives watch with a combination of disgust and pity. After the act, Baby Doll, who is thirty-four, sits in her tiny dressing room, like a little girl crammed into a doll house, and laments her predicament.

"I'm 265 pounds now. I lost the rest of it dancing. I gross $90 a week, but I'd rather sit at home and be a mother to my children. I've had seven babies and three miscarriages. The doctor says I have to lose about a hundred pounds, but if I do that I'll lose my job. What bothers me most is my stomach. Being so big and having so many children, I've never worn a girdle. Now I don't think my stomach will ever go away. Usually I don't take what the people out there say to heart. I don't let it bother me. Usually."

From the spectacle of Baby Doll, you can walk past the good-natured drunks, conventioneers riding in horse-drawn buggies, and wide-eyed secretaries visiting from Houston, and move into back streets without glare or noise, narrow streets under tall porches, with windows covered by green shutters that release tiny darts of light and touches of laughter and intimate conversation. The architecture is of old Havana, the setting still essentially French, in a time that could as easily be 1860 as 1970.

Across the street a thin girl in a white gown drawn in at the waist by a red sash walked onto the balcony and leaned on the wrought-iron railing. She turned and went back into the building, closing the tall shuttered doors behind her. She could, at the right time, have been a young woman from an up-country plantation who came to New Orleans on a steamer carrying cotton and molasses to visit a lover banished from the home county. Today she could be almost anything, in a city where almost anything is allowed, if it is done with grace.

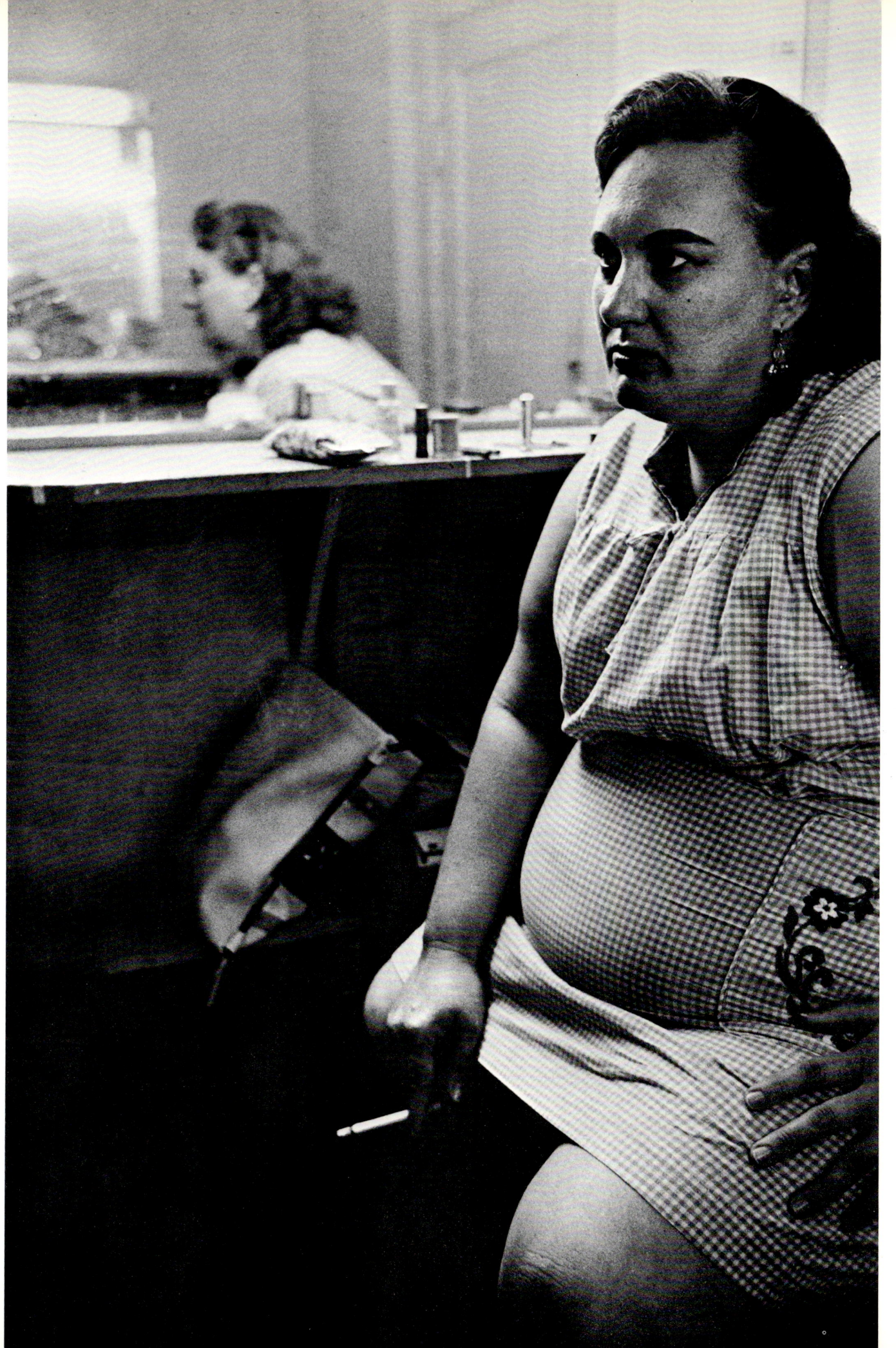

In New Orleans the Mississippi turns a soft brown color. It runs deep and wide, bearing ships of many flags, cargoes of many purposes. It takes on a slightly tired look as it passes the International Trade Mart, as though exhausted by being put through so many states and so many uses. But the appearance of weariness is deceptive; it is strong, and while many consider its journey completed at New Orleans, the Mississippi pushes on for more than a hundred miles before it ends its marathon trek.

South of New Orleans the Mississippi moves through a wide area where lakes and bayous and channels form a maze mastered only by those who have shown the ingenuity to conquer the "trembling earth." One early writer said these people were "aquatic men, with fins like fishes, noses like alligators, and feet like ducks." It is an area of homes and settlements, frequently on stilts, that cling to the few spots of solid earth. It is here that the pirate Jean Lafitte—bangles on ear lobes, a diamond brooch at his chest, glistening rings on his fingers, bowie knives at his waist—wheeled and dealed with an engaging arrogance. When the governor put a price of $500 on his head, Lafitte quickly countered by putting $1,500 on the head of the governor.

The people who now inhabit this region are fiercely independent and relatively untouched by modern America. Their forebears were Frenchmen deported from Nova Scotia by the British in 1755. Of the eight thousand banished at that time, nearly half died at sea. Some returned to France, others dropped off along the Atlantic Coast, but most who survived settled in this portion of Louisiana. Ignoring the enticements of New Orleans, they settled on the rich alluvial soil of the Mississippi Valley to pursue the ample fish and fur-bearing animals through the bayous and along the Gulf of Mexico. Like their ancestors, today's inhabitants are proud peasants in a rich but unpredictable land of beauty.

The highway that follows the Mississippi ends at Venice. From there one takes a launch to the last real settlement on the river, Pilottown, just above the point where the Mississippi shoots off into many fingers which probe and push through the accumulated earth to the gulf.

Pilottown is virtually raised above the water on stilts, with wooden walkways connecting its buildings. The town has neither a grocery store nor a church, but it has a bar, and also a school, where children can learn how to read and, more important, how to skin a mink. But the town really exists for the pilots who guide the oceangoing vessels between New Orleans and the gulf. River pilots take the vessels between New Orleans and Pilottown; bar pilots direct the boats between Pilottown and the gulf. The two groups of men have little in common except an uncanny sense of navigation and a rich tradition on the Mississippi.

Tim Flynn, a bar pilot for nineteen years, sat in the austere waiting room at Pilottown, glancing at the New Orleans newspapers and the *Wall Street Journal,* waiting for his name shingle to rise to the top of a rack which indicates it is his turn to take a trip. Commercially, the pilots' association is a cooperative enterprise, with each pilot owning a share. It is intensely inbred; apprentices are usually selected from the families of the forty-two men in the bar pilots' association.

Flynn and his colleagues talked about the mosquitoes ("big enough they ought to wear license plates") and the qualities of foreign seamen ("the Japanese have the best discipline") and humorous sea stories ("one of the Norwegian captains told me he and his crew had to read the works of Chairman Mao before they'd let him dock at one of those Red Chinese ports"). The men enjoy a quiet existence between shifts on the river—reading, fishing, and studying charts which trace the unending changes in the channel.

When a launch took Flynn out to a Norwegian freighter, he was all business. Dressed in a suit, white shirt, and tie, he was polite but formal. The beefy captain in a white uniform welcomed him to the bridge, and Flynn started the vessel down the south pass.

"Starboard 10 rudder," he ordered the helmsman. The orders were precise. "Midship . . . steady . . . dead slow ahead." Into a relatively uncomplicated stretch, Flynn chatted with the captain, who told him about an especially fine meal in New Orleans and then produced a camera he had purchased in Japan.

It is slightly more than twenty miles from Pilottown to the gulf and the freighter passes oil rigs, little steel complexes of workshops and storage tanks, houseboats for oil workers, a lighthouse, and an abandoned military base slowly being overcome by grass and vines. Flynn moves easily across the bridge, pausing to eat a sandwich on a tray brought to him by a plump stewardess. He points out a good fishing spot and interesting objects for the captain to photograph.

At the gulf a launch will meet the ship, and Flynn will be taken to another pilot's station, where his name shingle will be placed at the bottom of the rack and rise until it is his turn to take a ship north to Pilottown.

In the distance one can see the green water of the gulf. "When the river is dead low," said Flynn, "you can catch sea fish at Pilottown and get saltwater all the way up to New Orleans."

The green water was getting closer, and the launch sent to pick up Tim Flynn was running alongside the freighter. The brown of the river met the green of the gulf, but the colors do not intermingle. Instead there is merely a line—green on one side, brown on the other. This is where the Mississippi ends, and at its end there is a sadness. The voyage is long, the history rich, the people varied. The river has been used, abused, bridged, dredged, diverted, and too rarely honored. The Mississippi has been involved in the forging of America, a part of the nation's dreams and aspirations. The sadness, you realize, comes of witnessing a very great work draw to its completion.